SCIENCE FICTION MOVIES

PHILIP STRICK

octopus

INTRODUCTION

I think that landscape is a formalization of space and time, and the external landscapes directly reflect interior states of mind – in fact the only external landscapes that have any meaning are those which are reflected in the Central Nervous System, if you like, by their direct analogues. – J. G. Ballard.

The first step, and undoubtedly the most difficult, is to decide what is meant by a 'science-fiction' film. This book provides a whole range of answers, more by implication than by definition, and I had better admit immediately that the range is indicative of indecision rather than of a wish to encompass all preferences and make everybody happy. Science fiction is a vast subject rendered only more complex when translated into film.

At the risk of seeming to adopt an irrational approach to what should, on the face of it, be a solidly rational theme, let me explain that in my view the term 'science fiction' has curiously enough become its own definition. It's an experience which satisfies different requirements in each of us, although broadly we might all agree on what it *means*; science-fiction fans are as fervent as any enthusiasts in the recognition of their identity but are seldom to be found in agreement on any of the details. 'If I like it, it's science fiction' seems as close as one can get to unanimity.

H. G. Wells, whose influence lurks unexpectedly behind much that is in this book, called his own writings 'fantasias of possibility', an expression the more

pleasing for its relevance to *any* kind of fiction. The Polish writer Stanislaw Lem, however, has pointed out that the only way to progress is by abolishing formerly valid definitions, and since science fiction is concerned with progress there's no sense in expecting it to conform to a fixed pattern. The only constant thing about it is that it changes all the time. I like *that* argument too.

So let's bypass this hurdle for the moment, instead of tripping over it, and consider the next one: the identity of science-fiction cinema. In my time I have argued that this concept attempts to combine two entirely different species, and that film should not be used to study what is at its best a vivid literary form. But it now seems to me that in many ways the cinema *is* science fiction. It deals with unrealities in a mood of total conviction. It demonstrates alternatives and allows you to share in them. It is fantasy constructed around actuality, and the translation of ideas into images. It is a seductive illusion dependent upon scientific and chemical principles. Any film worth experiencing is one that hauls you inside itself for ninety minutes or so, finally to disgorge you in a state of dazzled rebirth, and the same applies, of course, to any reasonably competent science-fiction story.

Fantasias of possibility – Wells's phrase works even better in this context. For the paradox of the science-fiction film is that it carries its own contradiction within itself. A space wheel, for example, may not be orbiting the Earth right now, but *2001: A Space Odyssey* has actually shown us the thing in full flight, and with far greater clarity than the NASA moonflight transmissions were able to achieve. The wheel has *already* been filmed; after Kubrick, you might say, there seems little point in spending a fortune on the genuine article. If you want to know what it's like in space, the whole experience is made safe and easy for us by *2001*, preferably on the biggest screen in town.

If you want to experience nuclear warfare and survive, it's all there in *The War Game*. Want to see the effects of ecological breakdown and overpopulation? In *No Blade of Grass* and *Soylent Green* tomorrow has become yesterday, and we are still occupying our respective to-days, floating in a bubble of horrific 'now' like the girl in the glass phone-booth in Hitchcock's *The Birds*. The cinema creates its futures out of images filmed many months ago, which indeed increasingly show their age, like *Forbidden Planet* or *Things to Come*, and become history without ever having been fact. Although science fiction tries to cheat time by taking us ahead, it is subject to the same laws as the rest of us and shows us only what we know already, disguised and decorated maybe, but alien only in the sense that no two minds think in exactly the same way.

Increasingly one can argue that science-fiction movies are no different from any other kind, that *Earthquake*, for example, is science fiction and *The Terminal Man* a mainstream story. And those arbitrary examples, as it happens, illustrate another Lem theory – that the mainstream tells us now practically all about nearly nothing, while science fiction tells us almost nothing about all. But the simple fact is surely that science fiction itself has changed. Isaac Asimov says that he's now living in the world he wrote about in the 1950s, much of his fictional technology has come true, and what was once speculation has gradually turned into contemporary fiction. Writers like Ellison, Malzberg, Moorcock, or Disch have in the past few years turned out stories that we seem uncomfortably about to overtake at any moment. And in the cinema it's not so easy to use science fiction any more to put a label on a film and shunt it off into the realms of fantasy. What's so unlikely about *The Conversation* or *Seven Days in May* or *Duel* or *Clockwork Orange*? They're just as authentic as *Scenes from a Marriage*, *Last Tango in Paris* or *A Bigger Splash*.

So this book is an attempt to illustrate that the old boundaries for science-fiction cinema are no longer appropriate, even if so many of the old classics must still be discussed. And it's a book, not an encyclopaedia; anybody who wants a list of all the fantastic films ever made should get Walt Lee's incredible three-volume reference guide. They're all there, from A to Z, more than twenty unimaginable thousand of them. I can't beat that. But I *have* had enough of the interminable hit parade of the same top s-f titles, and this survey intentionally gives only brief attention to a fair number of standard favourites while drawing attention to some less orthodox favourites of my own.

The remaining hurdle is that of critical method. Since I spend much of my time arguing that we should judge what a film-maker or writer actually gives us rather than worrying about what we thought he was going to give us, it's perhaps inconsistent of me to make any subjective announcements at all. I'm afraid they turn up just the same, and I can only admit to good honest prejudice. But although I would accept that in many ways science-fiction movies can be even more appalling than any other unpretentious, hastily made, time-filling form of entertainment, I think that even at their apparent worst they are worth examining very carefully indeed. They have a lot to tell us, whether we notice it consciously or not.

Among the torrent of titles and notions which follows, I have aimed to identify firstly what a science-fiction film is saying, secondly how it says it, and thirdly whether it says it convincingly (in my view). Whether I agree with what it says or not is irrelevant. If the film expresses itself efficiently, logically and with beauty, I'm more enthusiastic about it – but even if none of these qualities are to be found I would maintain that it has a voice and the effort should be made to listen to it.

As Lem suggests, we may find that it's actually using a new, improved language for what it wants to say. And that it's ahead of us.
PHILIP STRICK

CONTENTS

First published 1976 by Octopus Books Limited
59 Grosvenor Street, London W.1.
© 1976 Octopus Books Limited
ISBN 0 7064 0470 X
Produced by Mandarin Publishers Limited
22a Westlands Road, Quarry Bay, Hong Kong
Printed in Hong Kong

WATCHING THE SKIES

A good lady in Pennsylvania recently attacked me for disbelieving in flying saucers, giving as evidence the fact that they were continually landing in her garden. They made, she added, quite a lot of noise—although the only sound she had definitely identified was 'a beautiful, long-drawn-out hallelujah'. Arthur C. Clarke.

(previous page) Patricia Neal meets Michael Rennie's friend Gort in *The Day the Earth Stood Still* (Fox, 1951).

(right) Occupational hazards: Nancy Marshall attempts to recover her damaged robot astronaut (Robert Reilly) while avoiding capture by aliens in *Duel of the Space Monsters* (Fox, 1965).

A girl lies on a tropical beach, radio softly playing, companion lounging in the shade with a newspaper. Stretching at the water's edge, she pouts and sighs as the ripples flow across her skin. Her partner, lumpish and irritable beneath hat and sunglasses, take no notice but sweats peevishly as the temperature creeps another notch higher.

Suddenly, figures appear from among the trees, stumping awkwardly across the sand in spacesuits and thick, impenetrable helmets. They carry weapons like flashlights, which twinkle with a high whistling sound as the man rises from his newspaper to question their intrusion. He disappears in a puff of smoke. The girl runs off down the beach, screaming prettily, and is quickly cornered by more spacemen among the sand dunes. They carry her away into the unknown.

It's a scene from *Duel of the Space Monsters*, and as an example of the popular image of what you should expect from science fiction, it's hard to beat. The spacesuit and the girl have always been in close proximity, although not necessarily one inside the other, and many fascinating theories can be constructed as to why this may be so. One suggestion, uncharitable perhaps, is that science fiction in the 1940s was written for, and

greater technology. They had massive brains and usually more than their fair share of arms. Authoritarian, positively even parental in their ugly display of brutal power, their one desire was to enfold the girl next door and cart her off to unimaginable delights on some unapproachable galaxy. If they couldn't get the girl next door, they'd settle for the Playmate of the Month. They were disgusting, which was useful because by comparison the male teenager could appear quite presentable and the girl next door could unite with him against the common enemy.

The science-fiction magazines that consistently published stories as lurid as their illustrations were not the ones that stayed in circulation. They died with reassuring speed. The stories that are reprinted constantly from the 'golden age' of the 1940s and early '50s, stories by such great masters as Asimov, Heinlein, Clarke, Bradbury and Van Vogt, rang with altruism. The future of the human race appeared more interesting then than it apparently does now, and both the writers and their readers (to judge from the vociferous letter columns) were concerned that we should all be well prepared for the miracles to come.

But the male teenagers who went into the cinema business, flourishing away on the proceeds of World War II, mostly continued to think of science fiction in terms of its packaging. The formula was simple, and audiences responded to it: the aliens (or you could call them foreigners) are after our women and control of the world, whichever comes first. It would be unpatriotic to imagine otherwise. And so the magazine clichés became the cinematic ones, and the movie books are unavoidably full of shrieking girls who clutch hopefully at tentacles extended in uncomfortable invitation by perambulating heaps of slime.

Not, of course, the kind of stuff to be taken seriously; the effect was one of long-term damage to the image of science fiction. Only gradually has the academic study of the subject come to be regarded with less than incredulity, as if the serious contemplation of alternatives were on a level with encouraging pornography. In the cinema, a science-fiction quickie remains an attractive time-filler for producers and audiences who've run out of ideas, and are prepared cheerfully to accept that the cheap and the ludicrous are the very essence of entertainment.

Well, perhaps they are, if films like *Duel of the Space Monsters* are anything to go by. Originally called *Frankenstein Meets the Space Monster* (although just about any title you care to think of would fit equally well), this one was put out by Fox in the mid-'60s and is a triumph of vulgarity that has been undeservedly forgotten – the girl being seized on the beach is a scene of humour and affection inspired by the same sources as are apparent in *Flesh Gordon*, made ten liberated years later. The story, more or less, is of an invasion by aliens on the prowl for girls, wanted for breeding purposes

aimed at, the male teenager for whom girls and space-flight existed in a parallel universe. The spaceship, not unnaturally, was a potent image likely to make both dreams come true.

The male teenager, however, also had to cope with his lack of practical experience in both areas. Confronted by the average girl, his movements became clumsy, his speech muffled; he might just as well have been locked in space armour. Small wonder that his girl could be expected to scream and run. He was the abominable in pursuit of the inaccessible.

Equally troublesome were those beings from another,

back home. Thrown in for good measure are a hairy
extraterrestrial called Mull, which sits in its cage
turning increasingly tetchy as the plot unfolds, and a
robot astronaut that goes berserk when accidentally
damaged by laser beams. There's also a beach-party
sequence, lots of rock on the soundtrack, and some
precarious pointed ears anticipating those of Mr Spock.
It's diabolical, but by Jupiter it's entertaining enough.

In general, the invasion films of the '50s took themselves desperately seriously, with the result that they are
almost unwatchable today. Of the many examples that
could be quoted, the most chilling is probably *Plan 9
from Outer Space*, in which a flying saucer descends on a
piece of thread to attempt (for the ninth time) the
conquest of Earth. Completed in 1958, the film in-
corporates desultory glimpses of Bela Lugosi filmed
just before his death in 1956. The saucer, which con-
trives to be rectangular when grounded, summons
Lugosi and others from their graves to help defeat the
planet; but since the zombies do little more than stagger
towards the camera and back again on a stretch of
wasteland in the middle of the night, their alien con-
trollers are speedily repulsed. There are tiny moments
of concern in the company of Tor Johnson, the blind
Tweedledum figure recruited from Lugosi's pen-

ultimate film *The Black Sleep*, but otherwise the film
gives the appearance of having been slung together by
drugged mortuary attendants.

To be enjoyable, a really bad production should be
prepared to acknowledge its faults, like *Invasion of the
Hell Creatures* (1957) in which little green men from
Mars use their needle-like nails to inject alcohol into
their victims but are defeated by the glare of headlights
from the cars of courting couples. Another spectacular
pantomime was *Invasion of the Star Creatures*, scripted
by Jonathan Haze (the fall-guy in many of Roger
Corman's films) whose inspired lunacy had the Earth
attacked by strapping wenches armed with monster
vegetables. If this planet ever does get invaded, the
aliens will have a lot to live up to.

The most resounding attack from space in all science
fiction is of course *War of the Worlds*, the novel by
H. G. Wells that first appeared as a serial in *Pearson's
Magazine* in 1897. Although far from being the only
story of the period to deal with the imminent destruction of mankind, it had a directness of narrative and a
complexity of implication which together have ensured its lasting impact. The Martian fighting machines,
symbols of colonialism, Darwinism, the extremes of
technology, and the menace of the oncoming 20th

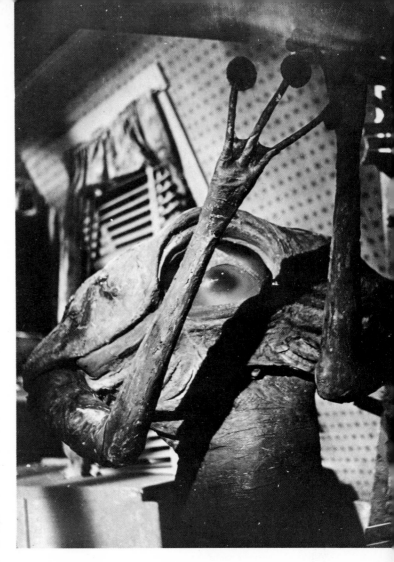

(left) Backseat driver: *Invasion of the Hell Creatures* (AIP, 1957). (right) Inquisitive Martian from *War of the Worlds* (Paramount, 1952).

century itself, seem to have stalked this world ever since. Originally illustrated in the pages of *Pearson's* by Warwick Goble, who saw them as tentacular lozenges mounted on angular pylons, they had become more like floating doorknobs by the time of their appearance on the cover of *Amazing Stories* in August 1927. And in the film made by Byron Haskin for George Pal in 1952, those charming tripod legs have disappeared altogether in favour of a cool display of antigravity.

Although Haskin's *War of the Worlds* can be easily enough attacked for its seeming disregard for the original story, an unbiased look at the film finds it not only superlatively well made technically but also moderately intriguing thematically. It opens with a brisk tour around the solar system as portrayed by Chesley Bonestell (who had already worked for Pal two years earlier on *Destination Moon*), demonstrating that the Martians only have one hope for survival – to emigrate to their warmer neighbouring planet, a mere 35 million miles away. These space shots are as magical as anything the cinema has ever shown us, even if Cedric Hardwicke's accompanying lecture has the hurried, shrill tone of an announcer persuading his audience not to leave. We are then plunged straight into the story with the first meteorite hurtling over a small Californian town, where the cinema is showing *Samson and Delilah*, and steaming in the ground as the sightseers gather.

One of these is 'the man behind the new atomic engines', Clayton Forrester, played by Gene Barry in his already immutable clenched-teeth style. 'If that thing's radioactive, we ought to keep people away from it?' somebody suggests. 'Might be a good idea,' agrees the expert, calmly. At a barn dance that evening, he has further wisdom to offer while, in the darkness outside, a piece of the meteorite unscrews: 'With the energy from just one square dance, we could send that meteor back where it came from.' Everybody looks admiring, a Martian heat ray blasts three guards, and all the lights go out.

From this point, the film follows Wells's lead closely by shattering all excuses for complacency. The Army arrives, digs in, and is flushed out. The Church advances, quotes Psalm 23, and is pulverized. The world's most sophisticated aircraft, the Flying Wing, not dissimilar to the Martian vehicles in shape, delivers an atomic bomb from which the invaders emerge without a scratch. An efficient montage shows 'the rout of

humanity' with documentary shots of ruined cities and crowding refugees. All too easily, civilization has fallen apart, just as Wells said it would. In the era of the Cold War, nobody doubted that it could happen at any time.

Nagging away at the need to re-assess our basic beliefs, Wells introduced the extraordinary character of the curate into his novel, and imprisoned him with the narrator in a ruined house beside freshly arrived Martians. Nearly insane with terror, the curate is clubbed down to prevent him attracting the Martians' attention, and this action severs the narrator's last link with conventional values. Dodging the murky implications of this chapter, the film puts Gene Barry in the ruined house with his girl friend, partly so that she can scream her head off when the predictable Martian tentacle taps her on the shoulder, and partly so that it can be established (contrary to Wells) that the Martians are absolutely unlike the rest of us. Everything about them, for example, seems to be in threes, notably the fingers on the groping hand and the glowing tricolour lens at the end of the serpentine metallic probe.

With the encounter in the ruined house, the film begins to resolve itself into a description of the struggle the man and the girl have to stay together in the face of inhuman chaos around them. When the girl is separated

(left) A couple of Gammians from Henri Lanoë's *Don't Play with Martians* (Fildebroc, 1967). (right) Jimmy Hunt contemplates one of the *Invaders from Mars* (Fox, 1953).

from him during the evacuation of the city, the man wanders in frantic search through the empty streets, a classic image to which the cinema has returned over and over again. Everything has gone, but that one isolated figure runs on through the wastes, refusing to relinquish hope. Charging grimly from one church to another, futile havens (witness a heat ray through the stained glass) of the last clumps of survivors, Gene Barry finds his girl at last. And as they embrace, the Martians come crashing down, destroyed, according to Cedric Hardwicke, by 'the littlest things which God in His Wisdom had put on this earth'. Genes, perhaps? Love, certainly, or so the editing must have us believe.

Wells, of course, intended his readers to be shaken, and his conclusion hinted at only temporary reprieve. Assiduous lover that he was, his romances providing only an elusive comfort, he would have been amused to find Haskin's sentimental ending so unintentionally close to his own, more cynical one. And although the film firmly discards his evolutionary hints, he would surely have approved of the atomic-age Martian holocaust, the more terrifying for a superbly compiled soundtrack. *War of the Worlds* deserves to be remade, many times. But the Pal/Haskin version deserves to be remembered, with affection.

Once Wells had drawn attention to the Martians, and since it became increasingly evident that the Moon showed no signs of life at all (except of course when UFO enthusiasts spotted fleets of spacecraft using it as a relay station; the Adamski photographs of May and June 1950 reveal the lunar equivalent of the Rush Hour), science-fiction writers and film-makers have speculated endlessly about the inhabitants of the Red Planet. As the place so clearly offered only limited prospects for survival and entertainment – other than boating up the

canals occasionally – it was to be expected that Martians would be set on reaching Earth as quickly as possible. Visits from Venus, paradoxically in view of the more mysterious, cloudy nature of the planet, were thought less likely, although in 1957 Nathan Juran and Ray Harryhausen brought back a large egg in *Twenty Million Miles to Earth*, hatched it into a 25-foot reptiloid called Ymir, and through the magic of Dynamation staged a battle between Ymir and an elephant in the Colosseum in Rome.

Martians were normally more sophisticated than this. In *Red Planet Mars*, released in 1952 while Pal and Haskin were still in the process of demolishing Los Angeles, the interplanetary theology of C. S. Lewis found curious expression through Balderston and Hoare's adaptation of their own play; Mars is not only Heaven (as Bradbury, too, once suggested), but is on the side of the Eisenhower Administration. God makes like a deejay, and Nazis, Communists, and anyone else who wants to argue, are given the push. By the 1960s, moral concern had given way once more to survival of the fittest, with films like *The Day Mars Invaded Earth* (1962), in which intelligent energy transmits itself by radio beam, duplicates all the Earthmen, and kills off the originals – a rare example of Martian victory.

In *War of the Planets* (also known as *The Deadly Diaphanoids*, made in 1965), the invaders are made of light itself, and have to be destroyed by that faithful team of Tony Russell and Lisa Gastoni under the guidance of Antonio Margheriti. In *Don't Play with Martians* (1967), they're the invention of a journalist who wants to tease the delectable Haydée Politoff (all too rarely seen after her spectacular showing in Rohmer's *La Collectionneuse*). The story becomes complicated by the arrival of genuine aliens, delightfully high-spirited types with cat-like eyes and pudding-basin helmets, fascinated by the rustic Brittany community where six of their infants are being born ('You must have come a long way?' says the stoical peasant behind the bar). They coo into shop-windows, get hypnotized by television programmes, and stay fit by playing leapfrog. As it turns out, they come from somewhere called Gammia and can manage without Earth perfectly well, thanks. No self-respecting Martian would tolerate such frivolity.

What Martians are after is control, and if they can't win by brute force they'll use stealth. In the same year that *War of the Worlds* appeared, William Cameron Menzies showed a more secretive alien attack in his remarkable film *Invaders from Mars*, which despite the celebrity status of its director (an Oscar for his design work in 1928, and international recognition for *Things to Come* in 1936) was later mutilated and is little seen today. Said to have been filmed in 3D (as was his next film, a disappointing melodrama called *The Maze* and starring a frog), *Invaders from Mars* gives more the appearance of having been made quickly and cheaply, using the television facilities where Menzies created most of his work from 1949. The sets are tiny, bleak and spare, and there is considerable emphasis on close-ups; but Menzies achieves an extraordinary depth with his use of lighting and colour, and there is brilliant photography by John Seitz (who also, by the way, shot *When Worlds Collide*).

Beginning with the statutory tracking shot through space and the arrival of a flying saucer in the middle of the night, *Invaders from Mars* shows how a small boy becomes aware that grown-ups aren't what they should be – starting with his own father (Leif Erickson) who has reappeared after a night in the sand-dunes with a small strange wound in his neck. In a series of placidly beautiful scenes, the boy watches other victims falling into the Martian trap, as if being converted to a new and tranquil religion; the local police, of course, are among the first converts. Only when his father is discovered

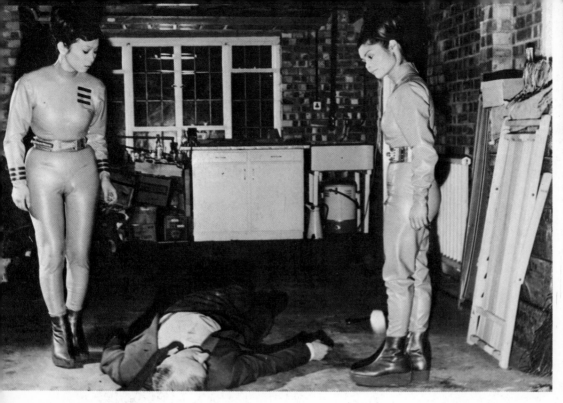

making an assassination attempt does the boy manage to enlist genuine help, and as soldiers blast their way into the dunes the film's tension evaporates rather briskly. Down below, green woolly Martians lumber about the caverns under the direction of a head in a globe; various shots of their pandemonium are used several times, presumably for economic reasons, while the shot of the spaceship taking off in a hurry is an exact reversal of its arrival. There are some massive explosions, and one small tree falls over.

Up to the point at which it turns into a charade, the film has a vivid and nightmarish quality (which fits the original concept, revealing at the end that it has all been a dream). The helplessness of the boy in an insane authoritarian environment was an ideal metaphor for the political paranoia of the time, and redneck zombies (not least those of *Easy Rider*) have patrolled the desert towns of the States ever since.

Another classic from 1953, also made in 3D, was *It Came from Outer Space*, which is more typical of the genre in that it was shot on location in Arizona, with real landscapes taking the place of Menzies' glowing, surrealistic studio. With Jack Arnold, the film's director, neo-realist science fiction came into being.

It Came from Outer Space was based on a Ray Bradbury treatment, and reflected the obsession in Bradbury's stories with the concept that nobody is what they seem. Aliens have made a forced landing to repair their ship, and recognizing with unusual tact that their physical appearance is likely to cause concern they take over some of the local townsfolk to act for them. The attempted discretion goes wrong when they keep making mistakes like staring at the sun without blinking, but once they've explained themselves to Richard Carlson who *hasn't* been taken over, they're able to complete

(above) Disposal problem: Yoko Tani (left) and Cali Raia in *Invasion* (Anglo, 1966).
(right) Escape claws: Beverly Garland in Roger Corman's *It Conquered the World* (Anglo, 1966).

the job without interruption. The moral, of course, is that we can get used to most things if we're sensible about them, and the unknown is just as likely to be congenial as to wish us harm.

The message didn't get through. In *It Conquered the World* (1956), humanity was getting it in the neck once again: rubbery bat-like creatures swoop down on Roger Corman's stock company and implant them with tiny radio receivers. Lee Van Cleef explains that this is an attempt by Venus to bring us to our senses ('You'll feel better in the morning,' says his wife soothingly), but finally discovers he's been double-crossed, and kills the villainous alien – a giant turnip with teeth – by roasting it with a blowtorch. Like all Corman's quickies, this one is rich with ideas, and the action belts along. One of the great scenes in all science fiction is the encounter between Peter Graves and his 'possessed' wife, who smiles an enchanting welcome and

launches a bat at him in their living room. 'A present for you, darling,' she laughs, and he dives under the sofa. . .

With *Not of This Earth*, made two months later in June 1956, Corman again had sinister humanoids attacking innocent bystanders. The alien visitor, identifiable by his heavy dark glasses, collects plasma for the folks back home, where radioactivity in the blood is wiping them out. Dedicated as he is to his mission (there is much screaming and macabre business with tubes and bottles), it seems an inadequate solution to a racial emergency. Aliens, to judge from the cinema, behave somewhat irrationally in times of stress.

In *They Came from Beyond Space* (1967), a Freddie Francis item based on Joseph Millard's *The Gods Hate Kansas*, stranded extraterrestrials again make the mistake of taking humans over by force instead of persuasion, spreading a lethal plague throughout Cornwall

as a side-effect. And in *Invasion of the Body Stealers* (1969), they hang about in the sky waiting for parachutists to happen along so they can descend to earth in duplicated form and make trouble for George Sanders.

In *Night Slaves* (1970), yet another spaceship is stranded and the locals have to be hypnotized *en masse* every night to come and put it right. Adapted from Jerry Sohl's novel and directed by Ted Post for American Broadcasting, this blandly efficient feature demonstrates just how masterly Jack Arnold's films of the '50s were. Although by no means unwatchable, it has about as much character as a parking meter.

Where *Night Slaves* is deflected by romantic trivia (James Franciscus falls for alien girl), the modest British production *Invasion* (1966) showed what could be done by stylish understatement. An alien on the run from the police of his own planet, Lystria, comes to Earth for refuge; unaccustomed to traffic, he gets run

Invasions of British cinema. (above) Dean Jagger studies the radioactive pit in *X the Unknown* (Hammer, 1956). (inset left) Martin Stephens heads the Midwich Cuckoos in *Village of the Damned* (MGM, 1960). (inset right) Marshall Thompson and Kim Parker are subjected to thought-waves in *Fiend Without a Face* (Eros, 1957).

over on an English country road and finds himself in hospital where Edward Judd and Valerie Gearon spot peculiarities in his blood test. Before they can do much about it, the hospital is enclosed in an invisible force field by the pursuing Lystrians, charmingly played by Yoko Tani and Cali Raia. The air inside the force field is slowly consumed, and the temperature rises.

A bit of quiet emergency shows the British at their best. In the era that began with the first Quatermass film in 1955 and ended with the third in 1967, *Invasion* was one of the few science-fiction movies not to contain an American star. Edward Judd, whose career at the time seemed perpetually bathed in sweat, was the British substitute, allowing the Lystrians to proceed with their own affairs – where someone like Brian Donlevy (best known as Professor Quatermass) would have grilled the lot. The film was directed by Alan Bridges (of *The Hireling* fame), sadly an infrequent name on the cinema screen, and it gave an efficient and timely picture of a community coming to recognize its distance from the centre of the Universe. In such a context, the Oriental features of the Lystrians carry an intriguing inference.

Possibly a sense that, from the Suez crisis of 1956 onwards, the future would be somewhat unmanageable, accounts for the popularity of the Gothic horror films made in Britain in the late '50s. Where the Frankenstein and Dracula melodramas wrapped themselves in the comfortable elegance of an earlier century, the ventures into science fiction displayed a consistent xenophobia. *The Quatermass Xperiment* vividly showed that nothing good would come of the space programme: Richard Wordsworth struggles back to Earth and turns with slow anguish into a mound of cactus. The sequel, *Quatermass II* (1957), demonstrated that aliens could be expected to take over the Conservatives, may indeed already have done so. Alertness and insularity seemed the prime virtues.

Aspects of Quatermass. (left) Richard Wordsworth comes down to earth in *The Quatermass Xperiment* (Hammer, 1954). (above) Andrew Keir and James Donald meet the five-million-year-old demons in *Quatermass and the Pit* (Hammer, 1967).

In these disturbing times, American know-how offered an essential element of reassurance. Dean Jagger dealt with radioactive heaps in Scotland in *X the Unknown* (1956); Forrest Tucker scowled resourcefully at such as *The Strange World of Planet X* (1957) and *The Trollenberg Terror* (1958), while Marshall Thompson blinked incredulously at the *Fiend Without a Face* (1957) and the *First Man into Space* (1958). Left to themselves, the British followed the example set by the Americans in that Freudian classic *I Married a Monster from Outer Space* (1958), and worried themselves silly over alienation. First their children became a menace, in the Wyndham-inspired *Village of the Damned* (1960) and *Children of the Damned* (1963), then their own wives, in John Krish's *Unearthly Stranger* (1963). To judge from *If . . .* and *Clockwork Orange*, the doubts and fears are still with us.

Nigel Kneale's third Quatermass script was his finest, and it took up the grand evolutionary theme that is one of the main thoroughfares of science fiction (recently embroidered by Erich von Daniken with some magnificent detours). In *Quatermass and the Pit*, the alien is revealed not as a recent intruder but as a significant ancestor, a source for myth, legend, theology, a dark force that may quite literally have been responsible for the ejection of mankind from his Eden of simian ignorance into a wilderness of knowledge and contradiction. Temporarily driven back in some cosmic battle, the force now lies beneath the earth recuperating, not so deeply buried that a new branch of the London Underground might not awaken it once more to take over the mind of Barbara Shelley in preparation for fresh conquests.

In *Quatermass and the Pit* the demons bear a faint resemblance to grasshoppers, but then the trouble with describing the ancient evil gods, as the horror-story writer H. P. Lovecraft discovered, is that they end up sounding like an entomologist's nightmare. Although Lovecraft made several brave attempts to give full details of the horrific beings that comprise his Cthulhu Mythos, he was at his best when employing indefinite adjectives like 'unspeakable' and leaving the rest to the reader. He also complicated his portrait of world history by having *several* alien invasions overlapping each other in the recesses of the past, so that different species of being could be conjured up in differing circumstances. The resultant confusion is sometimes exasperating but it can also be resoundingly powerful, as with *At the Mountains of Madness*, in which the frozen tunnels beneath a lost city in the Antarctic are the setting for macabre happenings of terrifying obscurity.

The cinema, traditionally expected to show rather than to conceal, hasn't so far been able to do justice to

Lovecraft, but Roger Corman and his art director Daniel Haller have made three honourable attempts, and there has been at least one dishonourable one – *Necronomicon*, made in Germany by Jésus Franco in 1968 and featuring a night-club dancer whose erotic performance embraces torture and murder thanks to the Devil's influence. And the French critics pointed out when they disbelievingly encountered it (the film is also known as *Succubus*), Lovecraft fans would be better advised to promote their cause by further screenings of *The Haunted Palace* – even though this superb Corman production, scripted by the science-fiction writer Charles Beaumont, brings Edgar Allan Poe into the act as well. Derived from Lovecraft's *Case of Charles Dexter Ward*, with Vincent Price giving a fine two-sided performance as the mild-mannered Ward and as his diabolical ancestor Joseph Curwen (occasionally both at the same time), *The Haunted Palace* (1963) is a distinguished film by any standards.

The Lovecraft village of Arkham, designed by Daniel Haller as a single mist-haunted street, lies in the shadow of the Curwen mansion (bearing a close resemblance to the House of Usher and other Corman/Poe hermitages), to which the village maidens are drawn as if spellbound in the middle of the night. As the film begins the villagers decide they've had enough of Curwen and they burn him as a witch, but the results of his witchcraft live on – pathetic, mutant beings, deformed and deranged. When Curwen's great-great-grandson arrives over 100 years later to claim his inheritance in all innocence, these other Curwen offspring encircle him and his bride in mute accusation until the tolling of a bell summons them away.

As we learn later, a repellent green extraterrestrial lives in the recesses of the Curwen cellar, its purpose – as ever – to further the cause of interplanetary communication, its method the slow but possibly pleasurable one of impregnating every available maiden in the expectation that a New Race will result. The plan seems doomed to failure, but it's lots of fun for everybody except the maidens, the latest of whom turns out to be Mrs Ward when her husband falls under the spell of his ancestor's portrait looming above the fireplace. Finally the villagers must intervene once more with their customary array of flaming torches, and the whole cycle begins again.

The extraordinary potency of what, in synopsis, appears arrant rubbish, is something only the cinema could convey. *The Haunted Palace* is constructed from smoothly swooping camera movements, a rich and liturgical music score by Ronald Stein, and vast, brooding sets – the greatest of which is a gigantic thick-beamed stairway down to the place of 'sacrifice'. We are spectators of solemn ritual, and it is performed with total conviction. But there are also subtler forces at work. Charles Ward, like other Corman/Poe outcasts, is struggling painfully towards sexual awareness,

his personality divided between retreat and aggression. The Thing in the cellar represents a truth he has to face, if he is to survive.

The alien, then, makes for a powerful symbol in science fiction of the forces we might prefer to leave buried but which will only cause us trouble if ignored. The alien has to be faced and absorbed, routed or destroyed. And it would be foolish, of course, not to expect him to return, so the skies must continue to be watched, the pages of the Necronomicon to be turned, with caution.

Lovecraft, for whom the world outside his head was always a place of menace and hazard, returned frequently to Arkham, and his admirers and imitators do the same. Daniel Haller recreated the place in one of his first ventures as a director, *Monster of Terror* (1965), equally irrelevantly called *Die, Monster, Die* in the

Lon Chaney Jr. and
Vincent Price attempt to
recover an old friend from
the vaults of *The Haunted
Palace* (Alta-Vista, 1963).

United States, which Jerry Sohl adapted from the
Lovecraft classic *The Colour Out of Space*.

The best part of the film, which suffers from a limp
performance by Nick Adams in the central role, is its
scene at the site of the meteor's landing, a silent yellow
crater set about with poisoned undergrowth. The
poison has spread to the nearby Whitley mansion where
Boris Karloff experiments eagerly with mutations
caused by the radiation from bits of meteorite. Finally
riddled by an overdose of radiation himself, he charges
around glowing insanely for a while before the place
goes up in flames. Perhaps it would have come across
rather better if the original story had been followed
more closely, but dialogue and atmosphere seem perpetually at odds with each other, and a similar awkward-
ness is apparent in *The Dunwich Horror*, filmed by
Haller in 1969. Dean Stockwell plays the schizophrenic

this time, Sandra Dee the lady marked out for close
embrace with the Ancient Powers, and Ed Begley
stands by to see fair play. The Necronomicon is fingered
reverently and there are a lot of coloured lights, but
what it really needed was a touch of the Mad Arabs.

The most memorable science-fiction movie dealing
with the resuscitation of aliens remains *The Thing*
(1951); in which a flying saucer is discovered in the
Arctic ice by the men at a US Army Air Force base not
far from the North Pole. 'A million years of history are
awaiting us beneath that ice,' they observe, but when
excavation begins the saucer explodes, bequeathing
them its solitary frozen occupant. Unthawed, he
proves to be a humanoid vegetable, setting a trend for
so many films to follow by living on blood and behaving
somewhat unreasonably about it. As in *War of the
Worlds*, attempts at communication are brushed aside;

21

(left) Silvia Tortosa meets the missing link, thawed out on the *Horror Express* (International, 1972). (right) Cultivating a taste for aliens: the blood-consuming plants grown from *The Thing* (R.K.O., 1951). (below) Nick Adams tries to dig the facts out of Boris Karloff at the wilting Whitley home in *Monster of Terror* (AIP, 1965).

the invader has to be burned to a crisp, setting yet another trend.

Directed by Christian Nyby, but in every way a Howard Hawks production, *The Thing* is as splendid to listen to as to watch, for the sheer pace and enthusiasm of its dialogue. As in all Hawks's work, it's a film about teamwork, with the monster and the glacial scientist heading the opposition and Kenneth Tobey in the John Wayne part leading our side. Contemplating the struggle with detached amusement, of course, is a girl (Margaret Sheridan), and if we continue for a moment to regard the alien as a symbol for pent-up passions the preliminary skirmish between girl and hero, in which she insists provocatively that he keeps himself under control, casts a fascinating light over the contest that follows. By overcoming the monster, he has a chance of winning the girl – but then he is also destroying something that has no emotions and no heart ('How superior!' exclaims the scientist), so clearly she knows what she's up to. The film ends with the urgent warning that more visitors could be on the way, although in view of the efficiency with which the creature has been dispatched, it is difficult to get too worried about more of the same. What in fact makes the film work so well is that the Thing could just as well be an escaped wild animal; all that's needed to contain and restrain it is clear thinking and prompt action. There's a splendid moment when someone opens a door to find himself staring the Thing straight in the chest; in many later films this would have been the cue for

close-ups of screaming retreat and a messy blackout. The Hawks man just shuts the door again, fast.

People retreat screaming in large numbers in *Horror Express* (1972) which, twenty years after *The Thing*, has yet another alien carved out from the ground and permitted to loosen up a little. Isolated on the Trans-Siberian Express, it forces itself through a rather complicated plot in search of knowledge, which it draws from human brains with such power that they are wiped clean and smooth (we're shown a few and, yes, they're unwrinkled). Its aim is to accumulate enough information to build a spaceship and return home, but the Trans-Siberian railway, subject as it is to bandit attacks by Telly Savalas, proves a restricted hunting ground despite the intelligent presence of Christopher Lee and Peter Cushing. Buried within the story are hints about the power of racial memory, but the action confines itself to zombie fights and brief, incredulous conversations, and the whole thing goes predictably off the rails at the end.

A well-loved image from *The Thing* is the circle of men marking out the dimensions of the dim shape in the ice beneath them. This was flying saucer time, an era that began with the Arnold report of 1947 and ended with a news blackout from 1954; within months of *The Thing* appearing, Adamski was meeting his Venusian in the California Desert. In 1952, there were reports that for three nights in succession saucers had hovered over Washington; the news had such an effect on the box-office receipts of that other great film of the period, *The Day the Earth Stood Still* (1951) that cynics suggested they were in the pay of Robert Wise.

Based on an obscure but timely story, *Farewell to the Master* by Harry Bates, *The Day the Earth Stood Still* remains the best of the 'warnings from above' type of science-fiction movie. Landing beside the White House and none of your nonsense about Tibet or the North Pole, a vast flying saucer disgorges Michael Rennie with an important message from 250 million miles away. As Kurt Vonnegut later pointed out, the message need have been nothing more than 'Greetings', the result is the same: aggression and bureaucracy prevent it from getting through. 'On Earth there are the forces of good and the forces of evil,' Rennie is informed by the Presidential Secretary, 'and we are the forces of good.' The alien treats that one with due scorn. 'I'm not interested in such foolishness,' he says, and loses himself among average Americans such as Patricia Neal in order to find, usefully, that Earth is not completely beyond reason. The White House never quite recovered.

Intelligent and unhesitating (it's worth recalling that Robert Wise was the editor for *Citizen Kane*), the film is also strikingly equipped with technical marvels, chief among them the huge robot Gort – the prototype, Rennie suggests, for a global police force. Similar mechanical giants have been lumbering out of space-

23

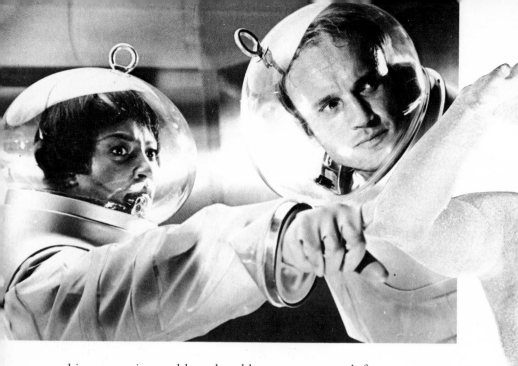

ships ever since, although seldom programmed for peace-keeping. In *Devil Girl from Mars* (1954) the robot Chani hunts for virile Scotsmen and finds John Laurie, while in *Target Earth* (1954) the Venusian robots imitate Gort in projecting rays from their heads but take the idea a step further and make the rays lethal. And following *Day the Earth Stood Still* (the title refers to the alien's demonstration of his superiority by casually switching off the world's power supplies for a while) few aliens were without their flying saucers. Ray Harryhausen modelled the best of these in *Earth vs the Flying Saucers* (1956), a pleasing drama creatively derived from authentic reports by the author of *Donovan's Brain*, Curt Siodmak; there were similarly creative 'documentary' shots in *Unidentified Flying Objects* and *Supersonic Saucer*, made in the same year.

It was the year, too, of John Mantley's *The Twenty-Seventh Day*, in which Gene Barry and four others are handed, on a saucer as it were, the means to wipe human life from the planet by telepathic command. Chosen arbitrarily, they are subjected to every kind of pressure to use their gift, but these aren't the paranoid non-entities from Malzberg's writings★, and once again Earth is permitted to survive. Only the wicked are destroyed, which, very certainly, Michael Rennie would have joined with the rest of us in finding hard to believe. With the approach of the 1960s, the aliens were increasingly inclined to give us up for lost, although with Jack Arnold's parable *The Space Children* (1957)

★Barry N. Malzberg, one of the most prolific and amusingly gloomy of today's science-fiction writers, is the author of the prizewinning *Beyond Apollo*, and such startling fantasies as *The Men Inside* (about miniaturized surgeons) and *The Destruction of the Temple* (in which the Kennedy Assassination is endlessly restaged). His works, written in so consistently a torrential style that they read like parts of a single book, are notable examples of 'inner space' fiction, which examines the processes of mental breakdown under contemporary events.

(top) Warned by nurse-technician Paula Kelly (left), James Olson protects himself from *The Andromeda Strain* (Universal, 1971) by allowing infra-red rays to burn off the outer layer of his skin (right).
(above) Intrepid astronauts Tau and Rho reach the ruins of earth in *Certain Prophecies* (Hungarofilm, 1968).
(opposite) End of an automaton: Ray Harryhausen's alien collapses in *Earth v. the Flying Saucers* (Columbia, 1956).

they made it plain that the next generation had a chance of saving us from the current one. Atomic warfare, said the film, was the sort of insanity only adults could dream up. For the following decade audiences were to give the closest attention to that appalling dream, and to conclude that Arnold was right. The skies cleared, and aliens don't come this way like they used to.

When they do, it's to run red-eyed through their paces, as in *Horror Express*, serving as symbols of the Unknown but never of the Unknowable. To judge from Robert Wise's *The Andromeda Strain* (1971), in which the lethal immigrant has dwindled to a mere micro-organism, there's nothing an extraterrestrial can teach us today. This beautiful and efficient production, described by Wise as science *fact* rather than fiction, is closer to a remake of *The Thing* than of *Day the Earth Stood Still*. Adapted from a novel by Michael Crichton, the most prolific science popularizer of the '70s, the film opens brilliantly with scenes of the victims of a virus brought back from space, and zips along like a thriller as the virus is slowly tracked down in the laboratory. With teamwork, brains, and sophisticated modern equipment, the menace is contained – and so efficiently

that the last part of the film has to be devoted to a largely irrelevant race against time to switch off an auto-destruct mechanism (irrelevant, that is, except in the context of Crichton's other work, which makes it plain that the greatest dangers to our survival are to be found in our own technology).

'Beyond doubt,' concludes *The Andromeda Strain* with a confident nod at the stars, 'other kinds of life exist in the Universe.' The time for being anxious, however, is long past. The Martian Heat Rays can hardly be worse than napalm. Aliens may even come and go unnoticed, no stranger than the creatures already occupying this planet. In the charming Hungarian short film, *Certain Prophecies* (1968), a flying saucer the size of a powder-compact releases its mouse-like astronauts on to a café table, where they gaze in horror at the ruins of mankind – the fish bones, the ashtrays, the crystal towers still glowing with dregs of wine ('This was the source of their energy'). As they return to the recesses of space, they pass a gaping waiter, and their startled radio message flashes across the galaxy: *Our predictions were correct. Mankind has vanished from the Earth. And the Gods have returned once more.*

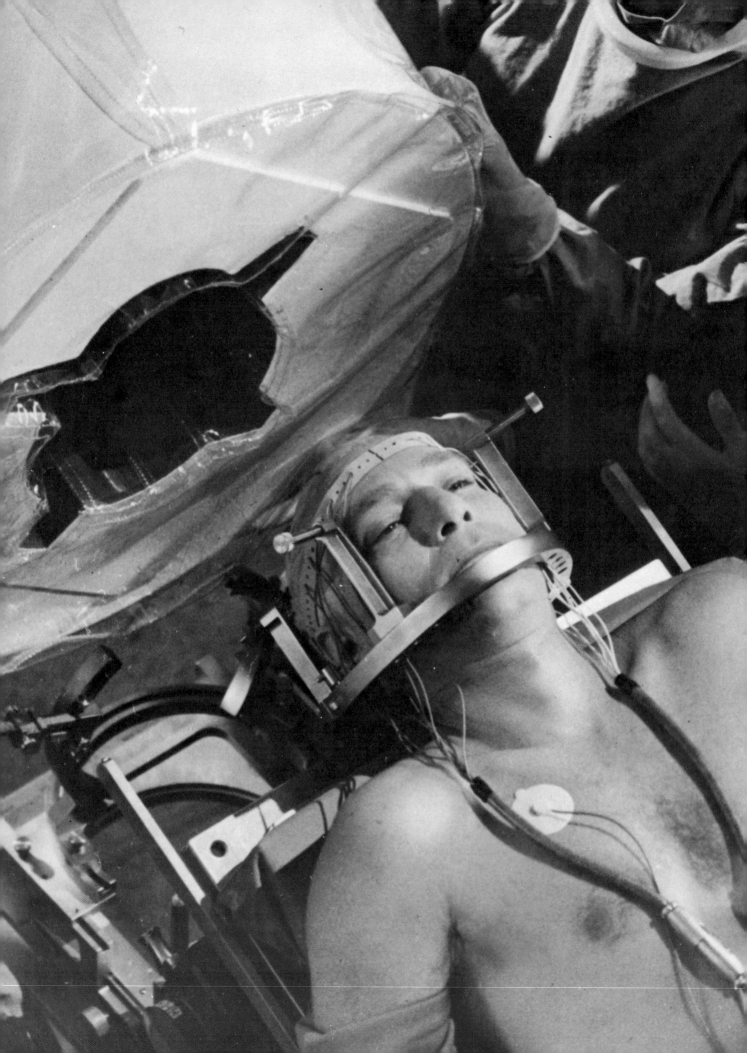

MEN LIKE GODS

Cursed be the day, abhorred devil, in which you first saw light! Cursed (although I curse myself) be the hands that formed you! You have made me wretched beyond expression. You have left me no power to consider whether I am just to you or not. Begone! Relieve me from the sight of your detested form! Victor Frankenstein.

The distinction between the horror film and the science-fiction film is frequently so fine as to be undetectable. Purists would argue that if it's good, it's science fiction; if it's messy and disgusting, it's merely horror. The horror film normally uses a sprinkling of technical apparatus, some electricity and test-tubes, in order to get its story on the move, but its main purpose is to stir the senses rather than the intellect, to arouse a gut reaction rather than a cerebral one. This is not to say that science fiction is concerned with Higher Things to the exclusion of earthly passions, but it is less likely to resort to images that are revolting for their own sake. The merely alarming is preferred.

Considering how little surgery is performed at the forefront of science fiction, it seems a paradox that the most important story in the whole history of the genre should be based on a medical triumph. But science-fiction writers are not in a position to describe 'how', except in rare cases of inspiration being added to specialized knowledge (as with Arthur Clarke and his satellites), and they are in any case seldom interested in the mechanics of the task. Confident that man can accomplish everything he puts his mind to, they concentrate on pointing him in the right direction or alerting him to the dangerous consequences of wrong turnings. If evolution is an upward path, leading to an ultimate perfection closely resembling divinity, we need to acquire a god-like purpose to accompany our god-like powers. In Mary Shelley's *Frankenstein*, the technical miracle of bestowing artificial life is accomplished within a brisk paragraph; the rest of the book, and, one might argue, all science fiction from 1818 onwards, is then devoted to exploring the consequences.

The creation of life is the most presumptuous, hazardous, and unavoidable of actions, even when only natural methods are used. And since the exact location of the soul within the body has never been satisfactorily established, although there have been a number of theories on the subject, it follows that a man-made creature cannot be supplied with a man-made soul. Mary Shelley's book allegorized the Industrial Revolution and found its mills potentially Satanic; more directly, *Frankenstein* took the struggle of *Paradise Lost* forward to the era of the generation gap. The Creature is Frankenstein's child, as well as his own, darker self. It anticipated Jekyll and Hyde, William Wilson, and the clone. And it, too, had read Milton, and could debate with its Creator on equal terms, an experience he found far from enjoyable. Yet the vexed question of its right to possess a soul left it incomplete, an outcast, a wandering militant.

The cinema is usually accused of having turned the story of Frankenstein to nonsense by the exceptionally unnecessary device of landing the Creature with a criminal brain. Certainly there were no Miltonic phrases on the narrow lips of Karloff as he wrestled with Colin Clive in 1931, and the many lurching monsters who have followed have consistently snarled and gasped and throttled with inarticulate anguish. But while the criminal element has perhaps led to a certain directness in coping with emergencies, the Creature's behaviour has never made it a figure of hate; it is loved rather than despised, its features caricatured endlessly in children's comics – where its readers surely recognize all too quickly the problems of ill-coordinated limbs and an inadequate vocabulary. Karloff and his successors, faces shadowed with despair, arms reaching out towards light, people, flowers, can't help but contain the pathos of Mary Shelley's original victim. Made stumblingly aware of life, they ask only to be allowed to enjoy it; repeatedly, they are refused. Burned, disintegrated, frozen, buried in swamps, they patiently await the next reincarnation.

For the Creature is never left to rest – he haunts us too closely to be ignored for long. In Paul Morrissey's hands he may be handsome, nude, and three-dimensional (*Flesh for Frankenstein*, 1974), in Mel Brooks's version he may drink, smoke, and break into song (*Young Frankenstein*, 1974), but even in the furthest reaches of satire he preserves an inviolable dignity – as if by his very existence he has survived and transcended the cruellest obscenity men could devise. He is at once the greatest achievement of human science and knowledge, and its greatest mistake. Like the cinema, he is closer to our mirror image than we can often bear to admit.

Although Jack Pierce's make-up for Karloff has become indelibly associated with the Creature, the screen tests when Bela Lugosi was being considered

(previous page) George Segal is computerized by brain surgery in *The Terminal Man* (Warners, 1974). Political humanoid (above) Olaf Fønss prepares to take over the world in *Homunculus* (Bioskop, 1916).

for the role were based on an already world-famous monster – the Golem, whose first movie was in the USA retitled *The Monster of Fate*. 'If you're tired of the Humdrum in Photoplay Stories,' announced the American advertisements in 1914, 'if you're yearning for something New in Motion Pictures ideas, you will be interested in *The Monster of Fate*. A real mystery story. A novel idea splendidly handled. A big problem worked out. Interesting to the last flash on the screen. *The Monster of Fate* is relish for the palate of a jaded motion picture public.' By 1914, it should be remembered, the public had been jaded by some of the greatest epics in cinema history, although *Intolerance* (the all-time greatest) was yet to come. The 'Humdrum' also included, presumably, the demoniacal fantasies of Georges Méliès, the first version of *Frankenstein* (1910), seven variations of *Dr Jekyll and Mr Hyde* (from 1908 onwards) and the entire *Odyssey* (1910).

Whether or not it was yearning for something new, the public was enthusiastic enough about *Monster of Fate* to require a sequel or two and to establish the fame of the monster's impersonator, Paul Wegener, who wrote and directed the film in partnership with his colleague Henryk Galeen (formerly assistant to Max Reinhardt). The arrival of World War I put the German cinema on a shaky international footing – hence the title change for the first *Golem* – and Wegener's first sequel, *The Golem and the Dancer* (1917) never left the country; but the third *Golem* in 1920 became a well-deserved classic, like so many German films of this extraordinary era (*Nosferatu*, *Metropolis*, *Faust*, *Siegfried*). Based on medieval legend, the Golem is made of clay, imbued with life by magic (the vital word is 'AEMAER'), and intended for use against pogroms. Like so many miracles, its qualities are selfishly misapplied and ultimately cancelled out by petty human desires; but unlike Karloff's more vulnerable being, Wegener conveyed solid contempt for his creators, and the gleaming malevolent eyes beneath his stone-helmet haircut implied a certainty that he would long outlast them. So far, the confidence has been misplaced – there have been no Sons, Daughters, Brides, or even Curses, although a Golem turned up in London in 1966 to embroider a horror story distantly derived from *Psycho*. Called simply *It*, and resembling a tree-stump in a strait-jacket, the Golem hauled Roddy McDowall's mummified mother about until it responded to the call of the sea. Then it sank like a stone.

Inspired by Wegener, the German cinema returned obsessively, from 1914 onwards, to the theme of artificial life. A six-part serial made by Otto Rippert in 1916 told the story of *Homunculus*, a sinister humanoid who moves into politics and ruins an entire nation as revenge for his lack of a soul. Like Cesare, the anguished somnambulist in *Cabinet of Dr Caligari* (1919), he was a figure that could be translated into a number of potent meanings, but where *Caligari* is habitually interpreted as a political metaphor, *Homunculus* is a morality play, a demonstration of the consequences of Godlessness (it takes a thunderbolt from Heaven to demolish the Anti-Christ). In both cases, the monster as a form of sexual expression is also implicit, particularly when Cesare drags the abducted girl across the angular roofs of Holstenwall; the famous expressionist sets of *Caligari* form a nightmarish landscape of instability where the conventional laws of behaviour no longer apply.

It was a short step to turn from hunting after girls to saving time, trouble and disappointment by constructing them in the first place. Where the Golem was short on sex-appeal, the robot in *Metropolis* (1926) was remarkably seductive even in shiny prototype form; remodelled into Brigitte Helm, it was irresistible. Fritz Lang's film balances two mechanical miracles – the sinuous robot and the giant, pounding furnace – and they are both man-eaters. With an insensitivity that is difficult to credit, the two most powerful men in the city decide that the one machine can service the other and that it will consequently no longer be necessary to maintain Metropolis's vast army of workers. They will all be replaced by robots ('in the image of man,' exults their inventor, 'machines that will never tire or make mistakes!'). But redundancy does not mean they can join the idle rich in the Metropolis playgrounds; they are to be tricked into starting a revolution and then punished by drowning.

The film is so astonishing to watch that the plot doesn't matter too much unless one tries to work it out afterwards. Its chief flaw is that when technology reaches the state of perfection implied by the architectural magnificence of the city, it is hardly likely to depend for its efficiency on exhausted workers pointing rods at light-bulbs. It is, in fact, an indigestible mixture of Victorian preaching and 1920s idealism inspired by Lang's visit to New York in 1924; and it makes more sense if one refers to Thea von Harbou's novel (created in parallel with the film) where the robot Maria is shown in effect as a resurrection of the inventor's wife who had been stolen by the Master of Metropolis and who died giving birth to his son. The inventor is thus rather more than a deranged scientist; he is, with good reason, a wronged husband intent on revenge and replacement. When the divine wrath inevitably arrives (he topples to his death from the roof of the Cathedral), it leaves the Master of the city intact, although he's as much to blame for the disorders of the past couple of hours. That's what you get for being smart.

In 1928, the star of *Metropolis*, Brigitte Helm, appeared in a film that again revolved around her unique ability to suggest evil and innocence simultaneously. Directed by Henryk Galeen and starring Paul Wegener, *Alraune* was regarded as so subversive that parts of it had to be reshot to pacify the British censor before it could be released, under the title *A Daughter of Destiny*. In this form, as a critic of the time pointed out, it was actually *more* subversive. The story is of a scientific experiment in which the seed of a hanged man is implanted into a prostitute, an early attempt at artificial insemination at a time when such matters were unimaginable. Haunted by shame and guilt, the originator of the experiment (Wegener) adopts the result – an unruly little girl called Alraune who is cruel to insects when young and makes determined advances on her foster-parent as soon as she's of an age to be noticed. Like the robot in *Metropolis*, she has an immense fascination; the scene in which, languishing on the furniture, she drives Wegener to distraction, has an unforgettable erotic intensity. The knowledge that she is in a sense an 'artificial' woman (magically created, like a mandrake) and his own property, and at the same time his accepted daughter, sets up tensions of desire that finally ruin both the creator and his achievement. Two years later, Brigitte Helm played the part again for a different director in a sound version called *Daughter of Evil*, but it served to prove only the brilliance of Galeen's production – and that the silent screen had powers of expression transcending those of the vocal cords. Based on a story by Hans Heinz Ewers, the adventures of Alraune seem due for revival; it's curious that she remains relatively unknown among the fans of fantasy. Her most bizarre exploit appeared in 1919, in a film called *Alraune and the Golem*.

The creation of perfect women appears a self-defeating pursuit since (to be partisan) there are so many of them around already, but Pygmalion and his descendants have always itched to work a few improvements here and there. If we are to accept Renoir's claim, the cinema's primary function is to celebrate as many beautiful girls as possible, their attractions increased by their inaccessibility – plus the fact that they don't answer back and never grow old. Renoir's own films, of course, illustrate this celebration in its most practical form, as with *French Can-Can*, in which a theatrical impresario genially grooms one starlet after another, moving on with urbane melancholy to new discoveries as each cycle of perfection is completed. A champion of natural processes, Renoir put artificial insemination into scornful perspective with his delightful *Déjeuner sur l'herbe* (1959), in which the plans of an illustrious biologist (a candidate for the presidency of Europe) to create an improved human race by genetic engineering are thwarted by a summer afternoon in the Dionysian company of Catherine Rouvel. She proves to his satisfaction that the human race is an ideal invention just as it stands.

When Frankenstein applied himself to a female Creature, urged on by Doctor Praetorius in James Whale's superb *Bride of Frankenstein* (1935), the result was the horrific Elsa Lanchester, hair standing on end like a Pharaoh's Queen who has just blown a fuse (and not too dissimilar in appearance to Praetorius himself, played by the angular Ernest Thesiger). Trying again, in *Frankenstein Created Woman* (1966), the Baron produced an immaculate body (Susan Denberg) but ran into the usual problems at the head end after inserting both a girl and her lover into the same skull. The result is fatal for several local males, until the Creature destroys herself in order to be able to think straight on a spiritual level.

Auto-destruction is clearly one of the risks of being immaculate, probably because it must result in a solitary and purposeless existence. Rider Haggard's passionate fantasies, *She* and *The World's Desire*, were sagas of adoration in which the unapproachable (which stood for the African continent as much as for womanhood) was shown to be endangered if submitted to the corruptions of mundane requests. The cinema has submitted the story of Ayesha to a host of variations, including a Méliès 'trick' film of 1899 (*Danse de Feu*) that was retitled *Haggard's 'She'* by its American distributor in order to improve the box-office prospects. In a 1917 version the second baptism in the flame of immortality turned Her into an ape; in 1935, the location was the Himalayas, and She had to compete for attention with a frozen sabre-tooth tiger; in 1964, the lady was interpreted by Ursula Andress, and in 1969 by Olinka Berova, confirming the time-honoured cinematic law that pneumatic blondes are more worthy of preservation than most.

Another magnetic blonde was Sydne Rome in Marcello Aliprandi's *The Tin Girl* (1970). Set in an indeterminate future, this presentable Italian comedy deals with the antics of a social misfit who breaks with the system by attacking his director's office in a suit of armour – a comment not so much on antiquarian work methods as on the mechanical nature of his employment. Miss Rome drifts by, Ayesha-like in flowing mane and robes, and shows a kinky interest in statues; the misfit pursues her, discovers that her armour is more than skin-deep, and disgustedly breaks her to pieces outside the robot factory. Then he has second thoughts, and the lady is reconstructed; a factory too, it seems, can provide the fires of immortality. Somewhat cluttered with Fellini derivations, and too self-indulgent by half, *The Tin Girl* is more a satire on advertising (where there are more perfect women to the square inch than Rider Haggard ever dreamed possible) than a serious comment on the future of facsimiles. But it's a modest advance on that British

(left) A heated exchange between Paul Wegener and Brigitte Helm in *Alraune* (Amafilm, 1928). (below) The kingdom of *She* (RKO, 1935) as conceived by Irving Pichel and Merian C. Cooper. Explorers Nigel Bruce and Helen Mack prepare to meet the immortal Helen Gahagan.

farce of 1949, *The Perfect Woman*, in which Patricia Roc is assembled by Stanley Holloway, crammed with difficulty into an armour of stays and corsets, and released to blow her fuses in a traumatic climax. It does seem that women are best left to their own methods of self-perpetuation; if the perfect man is so far beyond the command of science, the perfect woman must present a challenge too delicate to be considered.

Renoir's misfits, while showing some measure of genius (like the biologist in *Déjeuner sur l'herbe* and the impresario in *French Can-Can*), customarily earn only a disconsolate solitude for their pains, or at best become outcasts from society like the lovers in *Le Crime de Monsieur Lange*. His most disturbing example is found in *Le Testament du Dr Cordelier* (1959), a free adaptation from Robert Louis Stevenson's Jekyll and Hyde story; Cordelier, an eminent psychiatrist, tries to prove the existence of the soul by giving it a material form. When his alter-ego duly appears, of course, it embodies all the sadistic and uncontrollable qualities of his own nature, qualities which, as Renoir suggested as long ago as *Boudu Sauvé des Eaux* (1932), are not without unexpected merit in a sterile bourgeois society. It was a stunning illumination of an aspect of the Jekyll and

Women under fire: (above) Patricia Roc, Nigel Patrick and Miles Malleson hit the floor as Stanley Holloway's robot disintegrates in *The Perfect Woman* (Two Cities, 1949). (right) The stainless steel Sydne Rome in *The Tin Girl* (Italnoleggio, 1970). (opposite) Ursula Andress and the immortal flame in Robert Day's *She* (Hammer, 1964).

(page 34) Two scenes from Byron Haskin's *War of the Worlds* (Paramount, 1953), in which the Martian fighting machines rise from their crater (above) to terrorize the world, but at last are defeated (below).

Hyde theme normally overlooked; the polarization of good and evil denies the possible virtues of compromise. Cordelier's other half (called Opale) is like Frankenstein's Creature, the materialization of an ideal, and at the same time an escape from the boundaries of traditional laws. It is an extreme opposite to the extremism of Cordelier's own personality; where he is cold, restrained, cerebral, Opale is overheated, uninhibited, feral. Unable to tame or to tolerate this pulsing natural force, Cordelier kills himself.

In anticipation of an era when hard drugs have led to an orgy of deaths and atrocities, Stevenson's original story (published in 1886) was written against a background of ill-health and regular intakes of medicine. Although he literally dreamed it up, and aimed at no great moral statement, the book was an instant success, selling 40,000 copies within six months; it contained, evidently, implications that were widely valid, in particular the suspicion that psychoanalysis is a science of doubtful value. The test-tube offers knowledge, but not stability, whereas society prefers to consider itself built on habit and quiet conservatism. Controlled passions have always been better received than those held in check, except in one place – the cinema, the Mr Hyde of the entertainment business. There have been more than twenty films based on Stevenson's theme, their fascination derived partly from the spectacle of Hyde on the rampage but more importantly from the ingenuity of the transformation scene. In one version, Mamoulian's Oscar-winning film of 1931, the process – which featured the director's own heartbeat on the soundtrack – was so mysteriously effected that to this day he won't reveal how it was done.

Metamorphosis is an aspect of science fiction that presents no problems to film-makers. Méliès built his whole career on instant transformation, by cutting, by dissolves, by superimposition. He could decapitate, fragment and reconstruct his characters with a twist of the celluloid, although his example, strangely enough, is infrequently followed now that both make-up techniques and process shots have reached such remarkable levels. Like Stevenson, however, he revealed the chaos of uncertainties that lies beneath the human surface, uncertainties which insist on being explored and which lead, consequently, to scientific research. In pursuit of knowledge, Wells's Invisible Man finds that the defiance of one law leads to defiance of the rest; once beneath the surface, he has to stay there, a victim, like Dr Jekyll, of curiosity and ambition combined.

James Whale's film of *The Invisible Man* (1933), for which R. C. Sherriff and Philip Wylie adapted a script from Wells's novel, used the same tricks as Méliès had discovered in the 1890s, applied for Whale by the brilliant special-effects man John P. Fulton. When Claude Rains removes glasses, coat, and bandages to reveal nothing whatever, the experience is genuinely uncanny. Wells was pointing out in his story that

megalomania, too, is unsubstantial, but Whale evidently had in mind a light-hearted re-telling of the Frankenstein parable, and *The Invisible Man* is consistent with all his films in showing an articulate visionary at odds with lesser mortals.

Both Wells and Whale appear to support the view that science and instability are closely connected. Although no less rational, one supposes, than any other fanatic (any gathering of specialists, whether the subject be model railways or B-Westerns, reveals a fair crowd of eccentrics), the scientist on the cinema screen is usually the image of derangement. His one advantage, according to Isaac Asimov, is that he can be expected to have a beautiful daughter, although unhappily this is not obligatory. Repeatedly it seems that the level of intelligence necessary to make a major discovery (like invisibility, say, or a matter transmitter) can be attained only in conditions of grave discomfort and isolation, and at the cost of all other reasoning faculties. Eyes aglow, the inventor either seeks no more of his accomplishment than that it should add to the sum total of human knowledge, or proposes that it should be instrumental in securing his global eminence. How the Ruler of the World will pass his time is never too clear, but the theological implications are disturbing.

Mad scientists scurry about like clowns in the early silent films. The terrifying Doctor Tube, filmed by Abel Gance in 1915, is played by Albert Dieudonné (later to be a shade more calm as Napoleon) in towering cranium and squint. Tube invents a distorting powder which, incautiously applied, makes a dog long and thin and a couple of giggling visitors fat and wide. It appears to be of doubtful value to society, but you never know. Chiefly, it allowed Gance, who prided himself as a technical innovator, to experiment with the anamorphic lens. In 1923, René Clair made *Paris Qui Dort*, starring the Eiffel Tower and an absent-minded genius who freezes the city in the small hours of the morning; the citizens stand (or lie) about, trapped in positions of petty crime and self-indulgence, while those who have avoided the paralysis begin to celebrate the end of the world. The concept of moving at a different speed from everyone else so that they stand immobile, confounded by one's quicksilver brilliance, has been enjoyed in science fiction since Wells wrote *The New Accelerator*, but no other examples come to mind than *Paris Qui Dort* of this simple trick being applied to film.

Following in the wake of *The Invisible Man* was the inevitable *Invisible Woman* (1940) in which a tottering John Barrymore has trouble with the fashion model he renders intermittently transparent. The film was based on scripts by Curt Siodmak and Joe May, for whom 1940 was a good year; the same scripts provided the basis for *The Invisible Man Returns*, released at the same time and directed by May himself. A more important offshot of the original Claude Rains success was the breathtaking *Invisible Ray* (1935), a Gothic masterpiece

Tangling with science: (above) Boris Karloff demonstrates
Radium-X in *The Invisible Ray* (Universal, 1936).
(right) Tommy Kirk tests his circuits in *The Misadventures
of Merlin Jones* (Disney, 1963).
(opposite) James Mason reveals a new world to Paul Lukas
in *20,000 Leagues Under the Sea* (Disney, 1954).

featuring Boris Karloff and Bela Lugosi on equal terms.
Toiling in his Carpathian observatory, Karloff traces
the path of a meteorite from beyond Andromeda to its
touch-down in the African jungle. He excavates the
rock and becomes a specialist in Radium-X, which it
contains. But the price, as usual, is heavy. Karloff is able
to cure blindness, shatter statues just by glaring at them,
and kill at a touch, leaving phosphorescent hand-
prints; but he is not the popular man he should be, and
his mother finally destroys the antidote which is
necessary to keep him, Jekyll-fashion, in the land of the
living. 'There are some things,' the film reminds us,
'that man is not meant to know.'

Directed by Lambert Hillyer, *The Invisible Ray*
assembled a spectacular forest of gadgets for Karloff's
laboratory, reinforcing the popular view that large
quantities of glass, fuse-wire and tubing (along with a
substantial private fortune or generous sponsorship by
a drug company) are necessary for creative thought.
The film's hero-villain is also given that luminous glow
that interestingly signals his new status, as if converted
to some transcendental sect. In the 1930s, the halo effect
was relatively untainted by connotations of radioactivity; by 1951, when Alec Guinness appeared as
The Man in the White Suit, the shimmering whiteness

of his clothes made him less prophet than profiteer, and the effects of radiation seemed commonplace. Yet nothing establishes the unearthly faster than a good and ghostly aura, such as was applied by John P. Fulton to Lon Chaney in *The Electric Man* (1941), after Jack Pierce's make-up had been considered insufficiently disturbing. And nothing establishes the eccentric faster than a tangle of valves and coils, such as was carried to cosy extremes in the Disney comedy *The Misadventures of Merlin Jones* (1963), with Tommy Kirk developing a do-it-yourself electro-encephalograph in the privacy of his own home.

Whether or not there are things that man should know, there is plenty that he's not yet ready for, much of it described in the pages of science fiction. The most prolific writer about social immaturity was Jules Verne, whose books are dominated by stern philanthropists flaunting their discoveries to the world but refusing to hand them over. Awesomely repetitive and not particularly readable, Verne's books earned him a reputation thriving more on custom than on experience, but the cinema has treated him royally by maintaining the 19th-century background to his stories and emphasizing, at the safe distance of one hundred years, that he wasn't far from the mark here and there.

Best of the Verne films is *20,000 Leagues Under the Sea*, as made by Disney in 1954 with a $200,000 giant squid and a superbly reptilian Nautilus (Captain Nemo's submarine) designed by John Meehan. As Captain Nemo, the elegant manic-depressive recluse, James Mason brought qualities of forlorn intelligence that had already distinguished his portrayal of the Flying Dutchman; in the lavish stateroom of his atomic-powered submarine, madness and common sense engage in endless competition, a struggle that Vincent Price could imitate but not match in *Master of the World* (1961), in which Nemo becomes Robur, the submarine becomes an airship, but the story remains the same. Back in 1916, the challenge of *20,000 Leagues* was met by the Williamson brothers, the first to take a movie camera under the waves and create a commercial hit from underwater photography. The fascination of seascapes has ensured an interest in this kind of film ever since.

Arthur C. Clarke, confident that he'll make it into space during his lifetime, is settling for an interim substitute by exploring the ocean, where a wholly alien existence is to be found. The similarities between submarine and spaceship, between diving-suit and spacesuit, even between the cautious movements and the uncertain risks of both environments, are obvious attractions – but on an instinctive level the sea has a deeper, more dreamlike appeal, matching that of the cinema itself. Variations of the Nautilus are perpetually on the forage, from the Sea Crawler in the 15-part serial *Who Is Number One?*, directed by William Bertram in 1917, to the Hydronaut in *Around the World Under the Sea* (1966), a rather dumpy little container steered by Lloyd Bridges on a tour of weak points in the earth's surface. A 1964 Japanese version of Nautilus was called *Atragon*, and it could fly as well; its renegade owner uses it for scare tactics in the Verne tradition until he's upstaged by the Princess of Mu, the New Empire somewhat inconveniently located in mid-Pacific. He's then persuaded to challenge the might of Mu, which includes the giant sea-dragon Munda, but not before half of Tokyo has collapsed in the middle of the night, undermined by Mu-ites.

The city of Mu is a lavish setting, with sets and costumes worthy of *Cleopatra* and an equally enormous cast, many of whom get sprayed at the end with a foam that turns them instantly into statues (there's no shortage of ideas in Japanese science fiction). These scenes of ceremony and mayhem in the underwater city look as though they could have been taken from any of a dozen 'lost civilization' films, and will undoubtedly return – the theme offers plenty of scope for panic and pathos along the lines of the Atlantis myth. Unfortunately the potential is seldom realized; in *Captain Nemo and the Underwater City* (1969), Robert Ryan as Nemo has his hands full protecting Templemer from the sea-monster Mobula, while in *One Hour to Doomsday* (1970), a sensational cast (including Joseph Cotten, Edward G. Robinson Jr, Sugar Ray Robinson, Rosemary Forsyth, James Darren and Richard Basehart) is unable to prevent Pacifica from a deluge of boredom. In both films, large supplies of gold have a significant part to play. As always the sea is a great place for buried treasure.

At least three oceanic films deserve revival and reassessment. In 1926, filming began on an MGM production called *Mysterious Island*; it was completed three years and two directors later, in an intriguing two-colour system. Starring Lionel Barrymore as Count Dakkar, the film featured the customary giant octopus and sea-dragon, plus a charming race of little men with beaky faces and fish-like eyes. Four other versions of the Verne story have been made, including the 1960 effort with Harryhausen effects, but the MGM film, combining the talents of Maurice Tourneur and Benjamin Christiansen, appears to have been the most notable. The *other* Tourneur, Jacques, directed *City Under the Sea* in 1965 under the influence of Poe, Corman, Price, and Deke Heyward, with Daniel Haller taking care of the sets. Although hampered by David Tomlinson, this story of a grim hermit, whose life depends on remaining shut away from the sunlight he longs for, has haunting resonances overlooked at

the time of its first release.

Buried far deeper in the archives is Curtis Bernhardt's *Der Tunnel* (1933) in which Jean Gabin (in the French version) and Paul Hartmann (in the German) supervise the ultimate submarine trip – a tunnel beneath the Atlantic. To judge from the stills, the floodings, eruptions and disasters that haunt the project were stunningly portrayed; they appear in the better-known British version, made by Maurice Elvey with Leslie Banks and Richard Dix in 1935, but by this time the going was smoother (Elvey had already built the Channel Tunnel for *High Treason* in 1929). The original Bernhardt film, although cluttered with stirring expressions of support for the new Germany, is probably the archetype and is

certainly unlikely to have been bettered by *Battle Beneath the Earth* (1968) in which the Chinese burn their way under the Americans with lasers and have to be smoked out from a network of underground warrens.

After his successful direction of *20,000 Leagues*, Richard Fleischer tried his hand with a new kind of submarine. His *Fantastic Voyage* (1966) ventured upon the unfamiliar seas of the human bloodstream, and carried the magic of miniaturization to its logical limit—the shrinking of Raquel Welch to microbe size. As it turned out, she is less interesting, along with her companions, than the fascinating environment of tissues into which they are injected so that a master-scientist can be cured, from the inside, of a blood-clot

An underwater scene in the city of Pacifica from Irwin Allen's *One Hour to Doomsday* (Warners, 1970), also known as *City Beneath the Sea*.

in the brain. Crises assault them on all sides: the action of heart and lungs sets up remorseless currents, a pair of scissors dropped in the laboratory nearly destroys them with sound turbulence, and there is a fierce attack by white corpuscles like huge polythene balloons. Although the plot is a tedious matter of implausible sabotage, *Fantastic Voyage* is a film of authentic wonder in the tradition of *Incredible Shrinking Man* or, for that matter, Ulysses' encounter with the Cyclops.

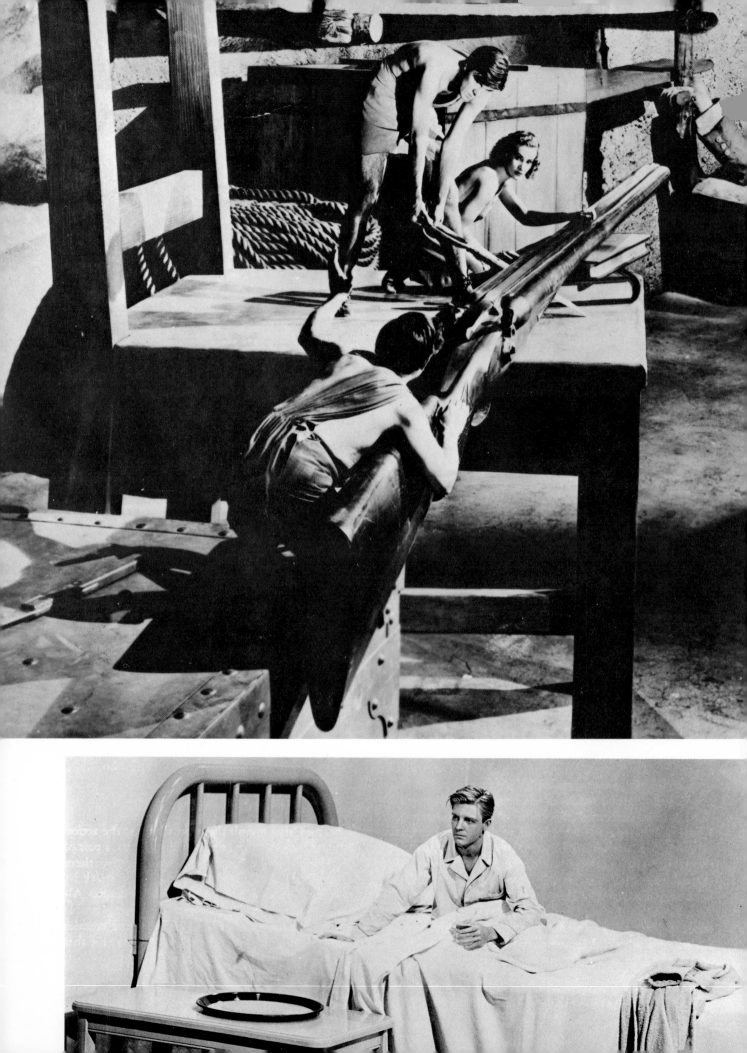

Differences in perspective: (above) The dwindling victims of Dr Thorkel (Albert Dekker) prepare to take their revenge in *Dr Cyclops* (Paramount, 1940). (left) Grant Williams finds the furniture no longer fits him in *The Incredible Shrinking Man* (Universal, 1957).

The Frankenstein complex finds a logical detour in the manufacture of mini-beings, such as are gleefully displayed in bottles by Dr Praetorius in *Bride of Frankenstein*, or farther back in the magical exploits of Méliès. In one of the screen's adaptations from A. Merritt's perennially popular novel *Burn, Witch, Burn*, Tod Browning shows a convicted scientist (Lionel Barrymore) exacting revenge with the use of telepathically controlled beings; this film, *Devil Doll* (1936), was the first to use gigantic models of furniture to suggest shrinkage, and the lesson was taken up by Ernest B. Schoedsack with his *Dr Cyclops* (1940). Daringly made in colour, and set in Peru where, presumably, it would seem more plausible, it told the story of one Dr Thorkel whose eagerness to test his powers outweighs all moral considerations: his guests find themselves dwindling rapidly, and although they too are scientists they greet the situation with antipathy. In keeping with the legend, the Cyclops is blinded – in this instance, his abnormally thick-lensed glasses are smashed.

The best miniature of them all remains *The Incredible Shrinking Man* (1957), the Jack Arnold/Richard Matheson classic in which the unremarkable Grant Williams sails through a mysterious cloud on a holiday voyage and begins at an accelerating pace to grow smaller. The story is simple but it generates, like much of Matheson's work, a mood of spiralling desperation and a complex symbolic charge. In an environment of increasing hostility – men treat him as a curiosity, the cat chases him, he is attacked by a spider in his own cellar – the man discovers in himself the resources for active survival. Like a hero on an obscure quest, his tiny victories actually increase his moral stature, until, still shrinking, he achieves an unexpected peace of mind and saunters out to meet the world of microscopic discoveries that awaits him. He is still, he reasons, one of God's creatures, and he might as well get used to it. It's a conclusion of dubious comfort chiefly because we are raised on a formula of wrongs being righted in the final reel, and the insecurity consequently lingers as it could never have done if an antidote had dropped from the skies. Matheson's parable, magnificently supported by the special effects, speaks of spiritual growth, and speaks with fear and reverence.

It set a trend, of course. Science was responsible for *The Amazing Colossal Man*, an unhappy event in all respects, in the same year, and there were *Attacks of the Puppet People* and the *Fifty-Foot Woman* in 1958. They followed the standard pattern: as a by-product of incautious scientific meddling, some passing human guinea-pig gets an overdose of radiation and goes berserk, becoming *The Most Dangerous Man Alive* (1958), *The Hideous Sun-Demon* (1959), or *The Beast of Yucca Flats* (1961). By the time of *Doomwatch* (1972) the nature of the poison had changed to meet the latest fashions, but the lumpy make-up and the irrational murders remained the same. Looking back at the 1940s, one finds that the stream of homicidal fugitives from science is so constant that the occasional shrinkage or gigantism makes a refreshing diversion; there was *The Monster Maker* (1944), *The Monster and the Girl* (1941) closely followed by *The Monster and the Lady* (1944), *The Mad Monster* (1941), *The Brute Man* (1946), and as early as 1942 Karloff satirized the whole routine in company with Peter Lorre in Lew Landers's *The Boogie Man Will Get You.*

It was folklore, rather than science, that ensured the popularity of these outcasts – the laboratory settings were knowingly located in Gothic castles. Even in serious science fiction movies, links with the Karloff era remain; Joseph Losey's *The Damned* (1961), for instance, conceals its sophisticated equipment inside a cliff, an ominous hideout controlled by a chilly and ruthless realist concerned not with people but with progress. His Creatures are nine children, saturated with radioactivity that should ensure their survival after the expected nuclear war; their plight is horrifying not only because it is so cold-bloodedly conceived and administered but because they have no future *unless* war breaks out. Thus, paradoxically, they exist as a justification for it instead of as a deterrent. When their existence is discovered by Macdonald Carey and Shirley Ann Field, fleeing from Oliver Reed's motor-cyclist gang, the intruders are allowed time to poison themselves before being hunted out to sea by a Government helicopter – in anticipation of Losey's *Figures in a Landscape* (1970).

Creating *The Damned* from an unsubtle book (*Children of Light* by H. L. Lawrence), Losey made a stylish and grimly ironic study of manipulation, consistent, as we can see from today's vantage point, with such cliff-top arenas as the Goforth mansion in *Boom!*, the essay in frustration in *Accident*, and the malevolence between one generation and another in *Secret Ceremony* and *The Go-Between.* He points out, as science fiction seldom bothers to do, that the right to pass on knowledge does not include the right to dictate how it will be used – or even the right to expect that it will be absorbed. It's important to be able to concede that the truths of one generation may be the lies of the next.

When the price of obtaining knowledge is so great, however, it isn't easy to relinquish or deny it. Although screen scientists can be expected to ask themselves whether they should carry on, this is just for form. They always do. In Mikhail Romm's *Nine Days of One Year* (1961) the physicist who has suffered an overdose of radiation has the opportunity to abandon his work and settle down to quiet survival with his wife; he gives it due thought, but moves doggedly on to his second, and probably fatal, overdose. Like the children in *The Damned*, he is a sacrifice, but at least the choice is his own. Similarly, Ray Milland wastes no time in becoming his own experiment in *The Man with the*

X-Ray Eyes (1963), testing out a serum that permits him to see straight through his patients and identify their ailments. Rather as with the 1947 Ray Milland film *Golden Earrings* (directed by the reliable Mitchell Leisen from a script by Abraham Polonsky), in which Milland discovers he's a genuine mind-reader, he quickly finds himself scraping a living as a fortune-teller. As the power of his eyes increases (a useful metaphor for the expansion of knowledge and awareness) so does his instability; he claims to be able to see to the centre of the Universe, although this proves to be rather beyond the resources of the special effects team, Butler-Glouner Inc., who have done a fine job in colour abstracts up to this point. Blinded and distracted by the intensity of his vision, he at last makes the most horrific sacrifice in all science fiction. It's the Dr Cyclops story again, but from the giant's standpoint.

Superiority is no guarantee of serenity, it simply puts you out on a limb, like Barry Jones in *Seven Days to Noon* (1950), hoping to bring London to its senses by threatening to blow the place up with the atom bomb he has been developing. Control over the actions of others requires a more direct means of influence, like the electric chair in Michael Reeves's *The Sorcerers* (1967) by which Boris Karloff and Catherine Lacey are able to enjoy vicariously the misdeeds of Ian Ogilvy. Under their increasingly lurid demands he is driven to commit murder while they watch, safe at home, in quivering ecstasy. When their Creature dies, their close identification with him means that they die too; miles away from his burning car, two charred corpses lie on the floor of their tiny flat.

In Byron Haskin's *The Power* (1967), hypnotism is achieved more simply as a result of what might be termed heightened evolution. A group of scientists involved in a research project on human endurance discovers that one of their number has developed superhuman qualities and is able to destroy by sheer will-power. George Hamilton has to work out which one of them is the master-mind, while his colleagues are killed off around him one by one: like the Invisible Man, the rogue scientist becomes an immediate paranoid. Handsomely and carefully designed, like all Haskin's work, the film has marvellous touches of horrific surrealism as the effects of telepathic control are shown by subjective camerawork, with walls and furniture joining, in hostile conspiracy to confuse the investigator, and there is a fascinating confrontation amid the glass corridors in which the shadows of the mind seem to be personified by the giant water-tanks hovering behind the protagonists. Michael Rennie turns out, not too unexpectedly, to have engineered the whole thing – but there's an unnerving twist at the end. Adapted from Frank M. Robinson's novel, the film has undoubted weaknesses like a spastic zoom lens, but it anticipates Arthur C. Clarke's Starchild (in *2001*) by some years in its attempt to show the implications of being the next

Looking ahead: (left) Ray Milland in Roger Corman's *The Man with the X-Ray Eyes* (AIP, 1963). (below) Alexander Knox instructs his radio-active pupils in *The Damned* (Hammer, 1961).

(left and above) Barry Jones goes berserk with an atom bomb in the Boulting Brothers' *Seven Days to Noon* (London, 1950).

(right) Michael Rennie and George Hamilton discuss the finer points of research in *The Power* (MGM, 1967).

(below) Vincent Price is awoken from his death in *Tales of Terror* (AIP, 1961).

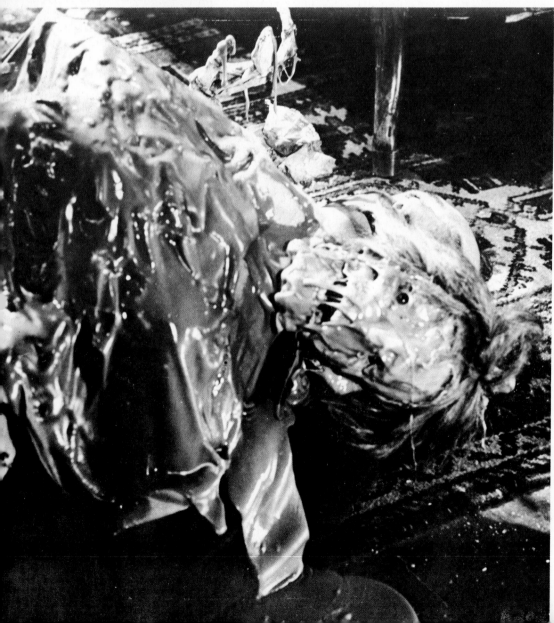

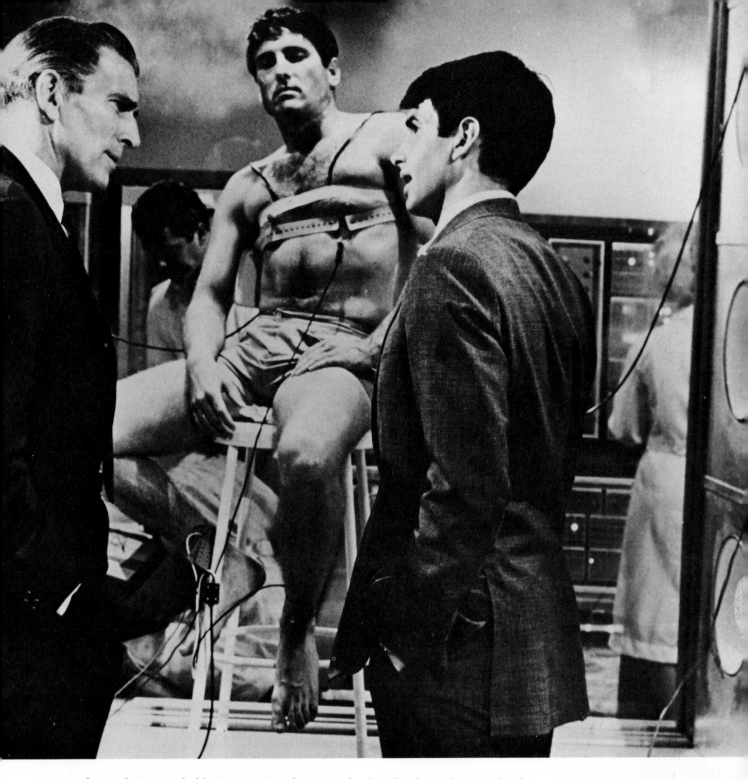

rung up the evolutionary ladder in a society dominated by those who haven't yet made it to the previous step.

As with *The Sorcerers*, which is the more memorable for being limited to a tiny group of strugglers, or *Village of the Damned* (1960) with its terrifying team of juvenile telepaths, 'mind over matter' stories seem to work best when kept to a domestic framework. The most celebrated yet simple narrative of the supernormal is probably Poe's *The Case of M. Valdemar*, which was briskly and effectively included in Roger Corman's tripartite *Tales of Terror* (1961). Basil Rathbone is permitted to hypnotize Vincent Price at the moment of

his death, and to order his awakening some weeks later. The cost of such an affront to nature is appropriately shocking, and makes a frightful mess on the carpet.

Control over life and death, with its supernatural connotations, gives the humblest medical practitioner a mythic status among the awed members of his local community, even amid the cynicism of the 1970s. In a classic novel by the Danish writer Valdemar Holst, surgery and brain-power are pitted against each other; the contest is the starting-point for a funny, frightening, and visually enthralling first film by Jens Ravn, *The Man Who Thought Life* (1971). A brilliant surgeon is approached by a man who claims he can think up living creatures, giving them substance just by concentrating his mind; he has got as far as mice but now wants to move to bigger things, and realizes that only brain surgery will release his powers to the fullest extent. The surgeon refuses to take him seriously, and the would-be patient, much insulted, proves his point by creating an exact facsimile of the surgeon out of thin air, his final masterpiece.

The copy is a great improvement on the original, and quickly takes over his career, his fiancée, and his life. The surgeon, to his consternation, finds himself treated as an impostor, unable to gain admittance to his own home – it's a case of Hyde being more popular than Jekyll. To restore order he has to masquerade as his alter-ego, a delightfully logical and potent conclusion to an intricate narrative. Although performed at times a little too much like conventional Danish farce, the film is spectacularly designed by Helge Refn and superbly photographed by Witold Leszcynski. Rather as with Krzysztof Zanussi's *Illumination* (1972), in which brains are sloshed about all over the place

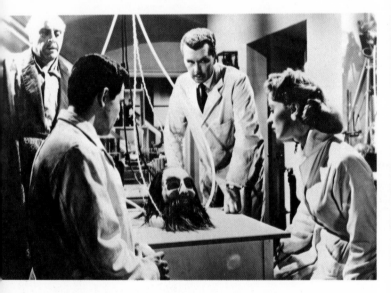

without anyone being the wiser about the way they function, *The Man Who Thought Life* confirms the paradox that the mind may solve the secrets of the Universe without ever revealing its own.

We have already noted that Frankenstein's troubles normally derive from malfunctioning brain transplants, the great moment in horror films coming as the mass of convoluted tissue plops into a glass container like something from a butcher's slab. In *Illumination* there is an appalling documentary sequence filmed alternately above and below a surgical sheet; below, the patient who is visible as far as his eyebrows mutters, laughs and groans, while above, where the top of his skull has been removed, his brain is thoughtfully prodded by a jovial therapist ('How do you feel *now*?') while audiences slump incredulously to the floor. Ever since Curt

Siodmak's *Donovan's Brain* was published in 1944, scenes have abounded in which brains float in preserving fluids, transfixed with tubes as if, like exhibits in a museum of technology, you could press a button and watch the wheels turn.

Relieved of the distractions of corporeal maintenance, their disembodied state appears to strengthen their powers and they order their keepers around like lackeys. In *The Lady and the Monster* (1944), Erich Von Stroheim gets taken over by his surgical miracle; in *Donovan's Brain* (1953) it was Lew Ayres, and in *Vengeance* (1962) it was Peter Van Eyck. In *The Final Programme* (1974), which required the fusion of the world's two most intelligent people – Jerry Cornelius and Miss Brunner – a brain was laid bare in order to demonstrate that all the technicalities had been considered. Since one brain looks much like another, there is possibly rather more shock-element in the spectacle of a detached head, with its implications of decapitation by guillotine, but in practice one either scorns the obvious fakery on the screen or gets diverted by trying to work out how it was done. In *The Head* (1959),

All you really need is brains. (far left) George Coulouris, Robert Hutton, Julia Arnall and the head of Nostradamus in *The Man Without a Body* (Eros, 1957). (above left) Preben Neergaard as the brain surgeon in *The Man Who Thought Life* (Asa/Palladium, 1971). (left) Jenny Runacre, Jon Finch, Basil Henson, Graham Crowden and George Coulouris in *The Final Programme* (Anglo-EMI, 1974). (above) Lew Ayres and Nancy Davis consider *Donovan's Brain* (Dowling Productions, 1953).

47

Michel Simon blusters and grumbles irritably on a tray while his former assistant (Horst Frank) puts the experience to good use by successfully transplanting a girl's head from her crippled body to a well-stacked replacement. The special effects are a great success but in all other respects the film is unbelievable; it's a considerable relief when Simon finally blows his fuses.

Where *The Head* was as disappointing as the film which had inspired it two years earlier, *Man Without a Body* (in which the head of Nostradamus is resuscitated to assist an American businessman), an unexpected pinnacle in these murky regions was Arthur Crabtree's *Fiend Without a Face* (1958), supposedly set in Canada but actually made at Walton Studios in England. Beginning conventionally enough with a series of mysterious deaths occurring in the vicinity of an air-force base, the trail leads to a nearby eccentric who is attempting to tap the latent powers of the brain and – thanks to some extra bursts of electricity – succeeds only too well. 'What have I unleashed?' he cries (echoing the anguished Morbius in *Forbidden Planet*) as the menace becomes visible; it takes the form of a whole army of brains with snail-like antennae and a stop-motion gait resembling that of Brian in *The Magic Roundabout*. Hungry for knowledge, these manifestations of super-thought suck their victims witless through holes punched in the base of the skull. Laying siege to the house of their originator, they hurl themselves through the windows in an extraordinary battle with the occupants, bursting into an obscene mess when hit by bullets. Despite its banalities, *Fiend Without a Face* sustains a mood of growing and frenzied panic worthy of comparison with Hitchcock's *The Birds*.

Although bouncing brains are perhaps in a class of their own, the concept of spare-part surgery morbidly intermingles pity and revulsion in the average heart. The pathetic, vengeful figure of the Mummy in horror films expresses the fear and fascination of hospitalization in its most direct form: the all-embracing bandages imply disaster, pain and deprivation, and at the same time a forlorn attempt to make amends. In the case of the Mummy, the illness they've attempted to cure is death itself, an affront to natural law that can only mean disaster. The search for an antidote to death continues regardless, updated from Poe through countless variations, including Karloff being injected with a serum of murderer's blood in *Before I Hang* (1940) and Burl Ives maintaining a whole community of spare hearts in *The Only Way Out is Dead* (1970). In Gordon Hessler's *Scream and Scream Again* (1969), one of Chris Wicking's more unrestrained screenplays has Vincent Price intent on a new race of super-beings made up of human odds and ends, and observing cheerfully: 'Man is God now – as a matter of fact, he always was.'

The art of rebirth has certainly been mastered by Vincent Price, as far as the cinema is concerned. After an engaging impersonation of *The Abominable Dr*

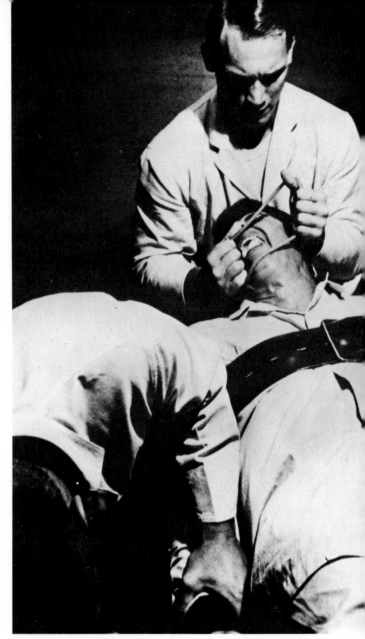

Phibes (1971), for instance, he was back for the sequel, his pallor flushed with a larger budget and a greater display of confidence at all production levels. In *Dr Phibes Rises Again* (1972), the skeletal musical genius seeks the elixir of life (which is somewhere in Egypt) to restore the wife he lost in a car crash. The film was directed by Robert Fuest, who was responsible for many of the more inspired excesses of *The Avengers*, and he whips the Phibes story along at much the same eccentric pace, even if there's nothing quite to match the re-run of the ancient plagues in the first film.

The script resounds with *Boy's Own Paper* dialogue, awful but effective: 'I don't think, I know' is countered, bang on target, with 'I don't think you know either, sir', while the demise of one expedition member who has been strapped to his bed and crushed like a concertina is revealed with an apologetic 'I'm afraid he had rather a bad night'. Gleefully re-using most of the Art-Deco trappings of its predecessor, this return to Phibes country also has a sense of elegance among its inspired

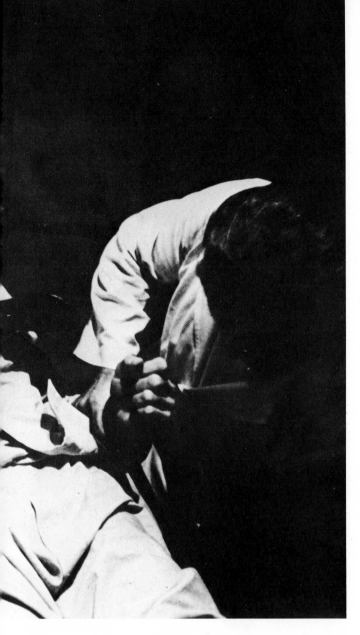

Rock Hudson is prepared for recycling in *Seconds* (Paramount, 1966).

absurdities (Hugh Griffith is packed off in a bottle marked 'Not Wanted on the Voyage', and a totally anonymous skeleton is greeted with cries of recognition). But Phibes's beloved wife remains unrevived at the end, floating off in her coffin to await further sequels.

Love can inspire many a medical breakthrough, as in *Four-Sided Triangle* (1952), when Stephen Murray loses his girl to John Van Eyssen and promptly creates her duplicate with various flashing lights and corkscrews in his barn at the back of the house. The experiment goes wrong, of course; since she's an *exact* duplicate, she too prefers John Van Eyssen. In Terence Fisher's *Stolen Face* (1952), a more primitive resurrection was attempted with the grafting of a beautiful face on to a woman criminal, but it works no better than the classic face-graft in Franju's *Les Yeux sans Visage* (1960), where

despite the amenable nature of the recipient the fleshy mask is horrifyingly rejected by its body. In *She Demons* (1958), an ex-Nazi tries to restore his wife's beauty at the cost of a succession of young girls, but it all falls through when the victims turn nasty.

The extent to which a new face will mean a new person has been debated for as long as age has left its mark on human beings. In the cinema, John Frankenheimer continued his contemplation of the difference between public and private faces *(Birdman of Alcatraz, Manchurian Candidate)* with *Seconds* (1966), a superb adaptation from the David Ely novel. An ageing businessman (John Randolph) pays handsomely for the privilege of appearing to die and being slowly rebuilt until he looks like Rock Hudson. Returning joyfully to society, he finds it even less tolerable than the first time around; he makes a complete mess of his new life, and pays the penalty of being hauled back to the clinic that resurrected him so that, like garbage, he can be reprocessed and his component parts used to make up other aspirants to rejuvenation. The manipulation of the individual by forces beyond his control, always an obsession with Frankenheimer, is here given an almost metaphysical implication, despite the cool, antiseptic clutter with which the theme is presented. The film is like a nightmare, in which the horrifyingly unalterable passage of personal time makes a deafening pulse-beat; for our pains, we are all made up of arbitrarily assembled components due for recycling eventually – whether we're willing or not.

After faces, hands are the most expressive part of the body, judging from the attraction of such films as *The Beast with Five Fingers* (1946). Peter Lorre was the almost obligatory star of this classic horror film, thanks to his memorable success as the surgeon in *Mad Love* (1935), in which he grafted hands on to Colin Clive (formerly Frankenstein, but now taking a turn as the subject of the experiment). The basis for *Mad Love* was the Maurice Renard thriller *The Hands of Orlac* (also filmed in 1925 with Conrad Veidt and in 1960 with Mel Ferrer); a concert pianist, losing his hands in a train crash, is fitted with replacements which had belonged to a murderer and which gradually dominate his personality. Peter Lorre, driven by his passion for the pianist's wife, is the evil genius who steers the pianist's confusion by masquerading as the executed murderer whose head has been sewn back on. They don't seem to write plots that way any more, although for a multiplicity of confused transplanting the Czech film *You Are a Widow, Sir* (1971) probably holds the record; featuring Olinka Berova, back home again after her Hammer adventures, it is a rambling comedy set in a future when heads, brains and other accessories are changing hands as casually as coins. The plot, however, seems to have belonged to an alien blood group.

In *Face of Another* (1966), made by the *Woman of the Dunes* director Hiroshi Teshigahara and also based on

49

a hallucinatory novel by Kobo Abé, the victim of a factory explosion is given a completely new face which he keeps secret from his former acquaintances, showing himself to them only as a patient swathed in bandages. In one form or the other, he hopes to win back the love of his wife and the respect of his friends, but it's a case of neither Jekyll nor Hyde being popular and he ends up with no identity at all, an invisible man in fact as well as in appearance. At the opposite end of the scale is David McCallum in *Hauser's Memory* (1970), directed by Boris Sagal from another Curt Siodmak novel, in which an over-eager research scientist injects himself with the vital compound RNA taken from the brain of a German physicist who has just died of an overdose of Russian secrets. In no time, he finds his head full of the physicist's memories, overlapping and confusing his own; these subjective glimpses of inexplicable faces, objects and events give the film a fashionably perplexing quality, but then it all gets bogged down in a petty revenge story as an ex-Nazi is uncovered and confronted. Susan Strasberg and Lilli Palmer are strewn, sadly wasted, along the wayside – but it won a prize at the Trieste SF Film Festival because, said the Jury, 'it was a fast-moving and well-made film in the best science-fiction tradition; according to many experts, this type of memory transfer may one day be possible'. It's as well to be warned that other people's memories may look like a Universal feature on NBC.

Two closely related lessons in the risks involved in playing God to the maladjusted are Ralph Nelson's *Charly* (1968), based on the omnipresent anecdote by Daniel Keyes called *Flowers for Algernon*, and the Subotsky production *The Mind of Mr Soames* (1969), based on a less-frequent novel by Charles Eric Maine. In both cases, a sub-normal 30-year-old is awoken to full consciousness and expected, with his new intelligence, to find a place in a world that has seldom been distinguished by its intelligent behaviour. In the case of Charly, excellently played by Cliff Robertson, the love of Claire Bloom isn't sufficient compensation for an existence filmed like a cigarette commercial; he tells his do-gooders that civilization is more interested in crushing the individual than allowing him to grow, and retires in injured solitude to regress as quickly as possible. With Mr Soames, played by Terence Stamp with the faintly puzzled expression that he put to such good use in *Teorema*, civilization as a whole gets no chance to make an impression; more the adolescent than the world-weary adult, he gets frustrated and violent when his well-meaning attempts at communication are treated with suspicion, and violence is what he gets in return.

It has been so often repeated that the disordered brain inspires anti-social behaviour that one would expect the cinema to find something else to talk about, but in 1973 the ill-advised zombie was on the prowl again in its turban of bandages. Actually, the film of Michael

Adventures in surgery. Richard Dysart (above) performs a unique brain operation on George Segal in *The Terminal Man* (Warners, 1974) but the patient goes berserk (below). (right) Two scenes from *Fantastic Voyage* (Fox, 1966), with Stephen Boyd, Donald Pleasence, Arthur Kennedy, and Raquel Welch being injected into their patient's bloodstream.

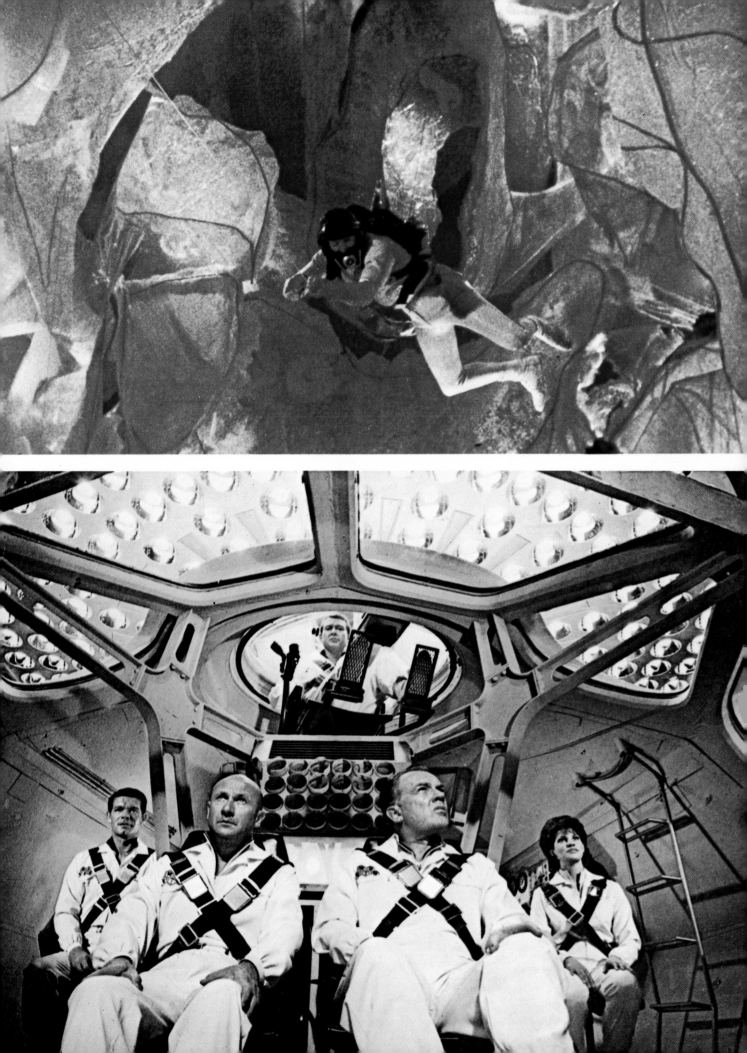

Crichton's novel *The Terminal Man* is something out of the ordinary, adapted and directed with admirable assurance by Mike Hodges and spectacularly assisted by Richard Kline's photography. Crichton's case, well documented with medical phrases, is so plausible it sounds like yesterday's news: a patient is fitted with a tiny computer connected to wires inserted in the brain, intended to nullify the homicidal effects of brain damage. But his brain, as usual, has other ideas – it finds the computer's signals so pleasant that it adopts a perpetual mood of violence just for the enjoyment of nullification. Its owner wanders the city in this malfunctioning condition, somewhat to the detriment of friends and acquaintances.

Hodges creates a mood of precarious efficiency that exactly matches the Crichton tone. In their crystal labyrinth of screens, monitors and mirrors, his hospital characters tremble with the unrecognized expectation of failure, checking print-outs like horoscopes before daring to operate. Their maverick victim is one of the four million Americans still behaving irrationally in a society where computerization toils for order and method. As orderlies snigger coarsely in the corners in the tradition of Frankenstein's imbecilic assistants, the brain surgeons posture with fragile arrogance, vomiting with terror before the operation, smug at its apparent success, and stunned when it goes wrong. On one level, *Terminal Man* is about vanity, its causes and its consequences. On another, it's a formal counterbalance between light and dark, with white figures posed against black or set down awkwardly among blocks of monochrome furniture, incompatible with physical or mental comfort, a background that reinforces the sense that man is gradually programming himself to extinction.

At times, as in the splendid tracking shot across row after row of television monitors on which the computerized Creature is describing his fears of mechanical superiority, Hodges is impressively precise in style. Elsewhere, as in the big murder scene, he simply seems to have tried rather too hard: a parrot trembles in its cage, an extract from *Them* whistles suspensefully on the television, a girl paints her fingernails black, and the killer's eyes snap open. It's clear we're in for high-gloss mayhem, and that's what we get – all splashing blood and punctured water-bed and fluttering rose-petals. In slow-motion, accompanied by Bach and rounded off by close-ups of the formal patterns of flowing liquid, the sequence ends in a kind of vulgarized beauty, fascinating to watch.

Adventures underwater. (above left) A crustaceous creation by Ray Harryhausen for Cy Endfield's *Mysterious Island* (Columbia, 1961). (below left) The remains of Vincent Price's domain in *City Under the Sea* (AIP, 1965). (following page) Under the influence of crazed computer banks, Robby the Robot turns kidnapper in *The Invisible Boy* (MGM, 1957).

With *Terminal Man*, monster and robot share a common identity. The operation that 'cures' the killer is shown in painstaking detail, a miraculous partnership between men and machines which fails not because either side betrays it but because the concept was doomed at the start. As the failed experiment lies in its grave at the end of the film and the earth is shovelled in on it/us, the fears of Mary Shelley are confirmed once more: create life, and you create death with it. But to create nothing is to live without meaning. You can't win.

The only consolation is the hope that the created life may represent a durable improvement on existing standards, that it will confirm the Darwinist theory by being stronger, bigger and more intelligent than its parents and will in turn direct life on to a higher plane. However, man is not yet ready to be outmoded, and cinematic robots, in obedience to Asimov's Three Laws,★ are traditionally servile, like elephantine washing machines. For twenty years, robots were a staple ingredient for the Republic serials, tramping about in vestigial tin faces and Chinese-lantern legs, impervious to bullets but vulnerable to electricity, girls and heights. The all-time favourite was Robby the Robot, the clownish mechanical butler from *Forbidden Planet*, who returned to star in his own film, *The Invisible Boy*, in 1957, in which his usual good nature was subverted by an evil electronic brain.

Where Robby, and even Daleks, are manageable bits of clockwork, the computer undoubtedly lacks charm. In *The Forbin Project* (1969), based on D. F. Jones's novel *Colossus*, Russian and American supercomputers join forces and take over the administration of the world. 'In time,' Colossus placidly informs its former controller, 'you too will respect and love me.' It's the assertion of every dictator, but from a machine it sounds even more arrogant. As with HAL in *2001*, we itch to pull out a few plugs. Robots should know their place, like the handsome specimen in the Russian film *He's Called Robert* (1967), who is turned loose on society and discovers like Candide that the rules are beyond its comprehension, or the resourceful Trent in Byron Haskin's *Demon with a Glass Hand* (1969) who carries the whole of mankind on a piece of wire in one of his fingers.

But Michael Crichton agrees with Colossus – the robot *does* know its place and intends to get there, eradicating inefficiency and illogicality in the process. Directing (for the first time) his own script, *Westworld* (1973), Crichton spelled out a powerful allegory about

---

★Isaac Asimov laid down the Three Laws of Robotics in 1941:
1. A robot may not injure a human being or through inaction allow a human being to come to harm;
2. A robot must obey the orders given it by human beings except when such orders would conflict with the First Law;
3. A robot must protect its own existence as long as such protection does not conflict with the First or Second Law.

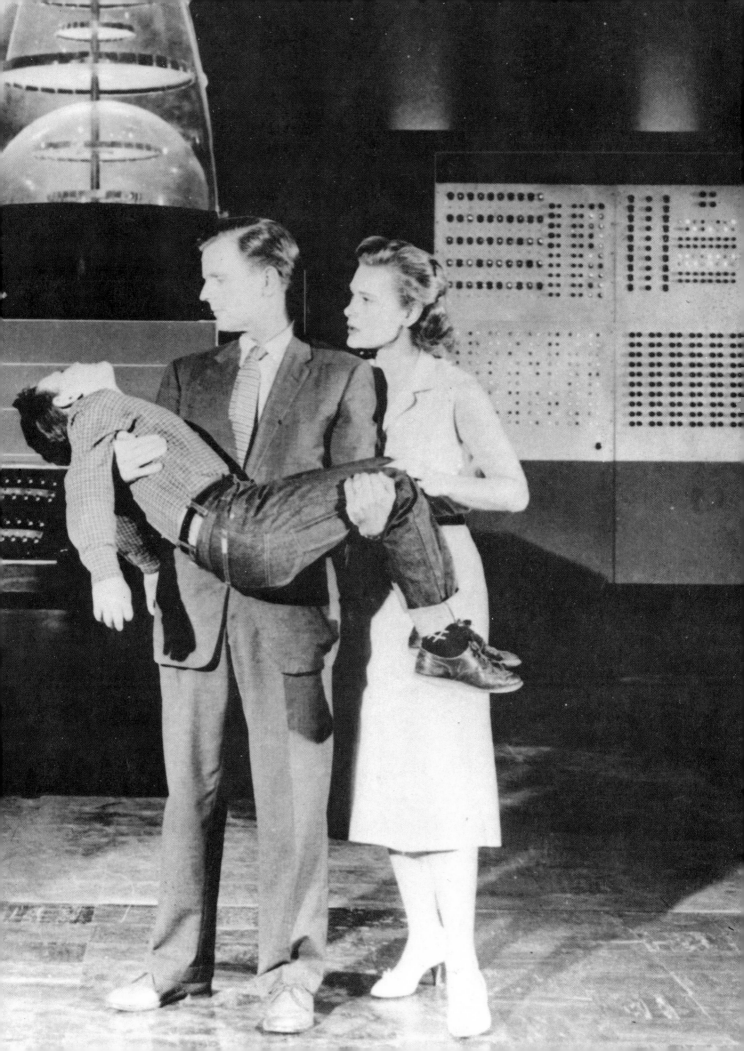

the myths by which we destroy ourselves, about the ease with which we dehumanize the society in which we live, about the evolution of man into a hyper-efficient fighting machine, and about the risks involved in externalizing our desires. With due reverence to the celluloid mirror in which men reflect their strongest passions and motives, hardly an image in the film's early scenes is not derived from the recurring visions of film and television – the eager interviewer from the washing-powder commercials, the expectant tourists being herded through pristine decor like characters in a Tati film, the massed ranks of screens and dials through which every action is observed and evaluated, and of course the whole setting of Delos itself, the holiday resort in which at least three kinds of dream have come true. There's Romanworld, an endless round of orgiastic feasting and merriment among flowing damsels and cool fountains. There's Medievalworld, where banquets and wenching give way only occasionally to the thrill of tournament or torture chamber. And there's Westworld, where the scrubby little studio street, the tinkling saloon and the rumbling stagecoach provide a background so familiar that the Wild Bunch could bust the bank at any moment.

'It's as real as anything else,' one idle tourist remarks to the other, a comment that could be extended to embrace science fiction movies in general. In Delos, everyone who isn't a tourist is a robot, which means that slave girls, Black Knights or gunmen are all programmed to satisfy the customer and fall at his feet in appropriate postures of impotence whenever he raises a fist. The black-suited gunslinger of Westworld spouts synthetic blood from the wounds inflicted by his inept opponent just like the dying men in Peckinpah films; dragged off to a workshop surgery overnight for some brisk tinkering with screwdriver and soldering-iron, his body is all ready to spout again the next day. He's both expendable and invulnerable, and as his circuits become increasingly sophisticated he gradually achieves, like any other offspring, a measure of independence.

What more logical, then, both morally and in terms of narrative, than that the robot should at last fight back, demonstrating his technical superiority over the feeble and inaccurate creatures who dreamed him up? Perfection may be the cause of the revolt but there's a hint of malice there too, of revenge for the indignities too often endured in the past. And so, headed by the expressionless Yul Brynner, the robots at the end of *Westworld* are all set to inherit the earth, leaving behind them the fragments of human caprice in a welter of bullet-holes, torn togas and fallen armour.

Lest we console ourselves with the reflection that humanoid robots are unlikely to be on the market in the foreseeable future, it's worth bearing in mind that mechanical overlords can take other forms. One of the Creatures that already has us in its clutches is the motor-

car, designed for our convenience and discreetly choking the life out of us. With films like *Point Blank*, *Bullitt* and *Vanishing Point*, Monte Hellman's *Two Lane Blacktop*, or even Antonioni's *Zabriskie Point*, the sensuous relationship between automobiles and the American landscape has been lovingly demonstrated to the extent that 'road' films have become a *genre* of their own. Their destination: an explosive anarchy, like the world of Godard's *Weekend* (1967), in which a dent in your car is sufficient grounds for shooting the roadhog who put it there. One of Godard's most intricate tracking shots in *Weekend* proceeds along an immense queue of cars, among which there are children playing, picnics being eaten, card-games under way – a kind of instant bourgeois community. At the head of the queue is the cause of the delay, a commonplace accident, blood and wreckage everywhere, uncaringly observed by the queue-jumpers. It's as if the motorists were queuing up to be demolished, one by one, meek supporters of an obscenely realistic Highway Code.

In Peter Weir's *The Cars That Ate Paris* (1974), the warning is even louder. The title makes it sound like a coy French comedy, but the film is Australian, and

Men like machines. (left and below) In *Westworld* (MGM, 1973) Yul Brynner plays the gunslinging robot, repaired each night for fresh slaughter each day. (bottom) In *He's Called Robert* (Lenfilm, 1967), Oleg Strizhenov (left) is the humanoid who takes over from the obsolete prototype.

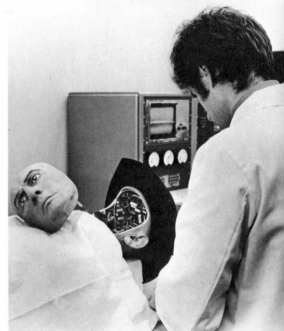

Paris in this case is an outback community not too distant from those little Western towns accustomed to remedial attention from such as Clint Eastwood. The law of the gun, however, has been replaced by the regime of the road, and the vehicles roaring joyously through the streets are close to severing all links with human control. Armoured mutants, so encrusted with chromium jaws and spikes that their drivers are lost to view, they lumber across the society that fostered and exploited them until it at last collapses. Paris has based its entire economy on road accidents, tempting the casual tourist into death-traps on the main road into the town. The spare parts and scrap metal are then used as currency, while any surviving passengers are placed in the care of the town doctor, who is much given to exploring new frontiers of medicine and whose patients quickly become little better than vegetables.

Told in a style of awkward humour, with performances veering from the competent to the makeshift, the film's suspension of conventional dramatic laws adds a curious potency to its theme; we find ourselves in an uneasy and uncharted territory where logic has taken a blind turning and there is no escape route. 'Gosh, Lord,' says the Vicar of Paris, presiding over yet another funeral, 'sometimes your ways are downright incomprehensible.' And by the time the town's adopted son is speeding off in search of fresh battles, the cars have devoured everything and we know exactly what he means. As with Kurosawa's *Dodeska Den*, with its pathetic community living in automobile relics, the machines symbolize more than our personalities. They symbolize our extinction.

If the Creature is to win, however, it won't be without a struggle. Steven Spielberg's *Duel* (1972) restages the contest magnificently with its account of an inoffensive travelling salesman (Dennis Weaver) who inadvertently falls foul of a giant truck and gets chased in his car all over the California highway. He never manages to see the truck-driver, and neither do we – what matters is the truck itself, a ferocious juggernaut snarling with fumes and menace, edging him into the oncoming traffic, hunting him downhill at 100 mph, and heaving him on to a level-crossing as a train goes by. Based on a story by Richard Matheson, *Duel* has all the Matheson character-

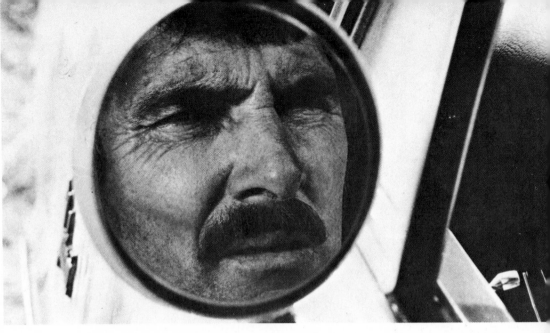

Symbols of extinction:
(above) Dennis Weaver is
hunted down by a truck in
Duel (Universal, 1972).
(left) Mireille Darc and
Jean Yanne barely survive a
car-smash in *Weekend*
(CCL/Ascot, 1967). (below)
One of the lethal vehicles
in *The Cars that Ate Paris*
(Aust. Film Dev. Corp.,
1974).

istics: an atmosphere of unmotivated but inescapable
malice, a central character unstable enough to be
imagining the whole thing and a narrative hysteria that
mounts steadily from an already paranoid altitude. The
plot is ridiculously simple, which makes it a convenient
symbol for any number of interpretations, but when, at
the end, the cornered salesman turns his car for a
showdown, wedging the accelerator with a rock and
standing by as the vehicles hurl themselves together
like dinosaurs, the separate identity of man and machine
is stridently confirmed. Sitting disconsolately at their
graveside, spectator to forces beyond his comprehension, the man has been granted temporary respite
but his survival is in the balance. The new Gods have
been testing their strength, and soon they'll require
another sacrifice.

THE MARK OF THE BEAST

Though I do not expect that the terror of that Island will ever altogether leave me, at most times it lies far in the back of my mind, a mere distant cloud, a memory and a faint distrust; but there are times when the little cloud spreads until it obscures the whole sky. Then I look about me at my fellow-men. And I go in fear.
Edward Prendick.

Although so much science fiction illustrates the talent of the human race for technical wizardry, this confidence of superiority over all other life-forms on the planet is put to the test so frequently that it appears misplaced. If the human intellect contains any elements of the divine, it is subjected to the constant challenge of the bestial, and the struggle is faithfully recorded by the cinema. No other art-form has produced a comparable flow of images from the twilight zone between man and beast, confronting each other at all levels and in all moods. On the one hand, our lovable feathered/furry friends, going through their tricks like circus entertainers, demonstrate a cosy symbiotic reliance on the ways and whims of mankind (*Ring of Bright Water*, *Born Free*, and the exploits of Lassie or Trigger and their kin). On the other, Nature demands revenge for continuing centuries of slaughter and misappropriation, and giant materializations of collective guilt advance on the muzzles of our flamethrowers. Haunted by insecurity, we need to see them attacking to justify our state of readiness, and we need to see them defeated to confirm we can still cope with anything the future cares to throw.

Our lives are pursued in an uneasy balance between transcending animal behaviour and sinking beneath it, a contest between sophistication and instinct being staged as man progresses from a primeval origin to a potentially sublime, or disastrous, future. H. G. Wells

was seldom confident about the long-term prospects, and in *The Island of Dr Moreau* he sets out good reasons for disquiet; rather than a horror story about vivisection, the novel is about the agony, and the futility, of acquiring knowledge, awareness, and an artificial social code. When Moreau plays God to the Beast Men, it is with no more purpose than to sculpt their flesh, to 'find out the extreme limit of plasticity in a living shape'. His Island is littered with failures who at last in desperation and pain renounce and destroy their deity (the Commandments are easier to break than to obey). But the sense of an elusive higher purpose still lurks within them, and a paradise lost calls out, obscurely, to be regained.

'The study of Nature makes a man at last as remorseless as Nature,' says Moreau, and his dispassionate shadow overlaps that of Frankenstein in the cinema's ranks of scalpel-bearers. Where Frankenstein is con-

An affair of the flesh:
Charles Laughton directs
one of the Beast Men in
Island of Lost Souls
(Paramount, 1933).

stantly returning in person, however, Moreau has never been permitted to recover from being torn apart by his experiments, and his successors seldom breathe his name. His dark reputation for extremes of brutality against animals further limits his box-office appeal. Even when he first appeared on the screen in 1913, Moreau was disguised as a Dr Wagner, and his work involved the local natives, their blood flowing under the door of the startled castaway who is the doctor's (white) guest. The film was called *Island of Terror*, perpetuating the image that linked Wells with Ballantyne, Stevenson, and a host of other 19th-century romantic novelists who pictured the isolated communities of the South Seas as hotbeds of beauty and bloodshed. On that same Island in due course were to be found Lord Greystoke (also known as Tarzan, and first revealed in 1912 in the October issue of 'All-Story' Magazine), King Kong, and the Lord of the Flies.

When sighted in 1932, it was called *The Island of Lost Souls*, its landlord played by Charles Laughton, and the chief Beast by Bela Lugosi; the script by Waldemar Young and Philip Wylie introduced Lota the Panther Woman, whom Moreau plans to mate with shipwrecked Richard Arlen. Wells was outraged by the changes, and the British censor gave him unexpected support by banning the whole film, but its modest reputation has slowly improved over the years partly thanks to ardent championing by French critics of its director, Erle C. Kenton. Today it comes across as perhaps the most successful of all the screen adaptations from Wells's work, for all that Laughton does his utmost to portray Moreau's depravity as very much an affair of the flesh. His nightmarish death beneath the scalpels of his former victims is one of the great horrific scenes in all cinema.

Kenton was originally one of Mack Sennett's

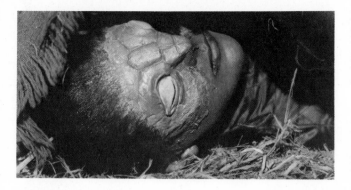

Snake charmers: (left) Maria Montez in *Cobra Woman* (Universal, 1944) and (above) Jacqueline Pearce in *The Reptile* (Hammer, 1966).

team, later to direct Abbott and Costello and episodes in Capra's *Why We Fight* series. He was an infrequent visitor to the realms of horror, but returned to them ten years after *Lost Souls* to make a couple of Frankenstein films and a *House of Dracula* (1945), the last of Universal's memorable series. Shooting *Island of Lost Souls* on location off the coast of California, he achieved an extraordinary atmosphere of hot-house menace, with the whip-cracking Laughton as animal-like as his flock.

In the same year, Leslie Banks let loose Fay Wray on *his* island in *The Most Dangerous Game*, based on Richard Connell's story *The Hounds of Zaroff* in which humans and animals become indistinguishable in the eyes of an insane Russian trophy-hunter. His trophy room, with its ranks of severed heads, was again too much for the British censor, who was having a bad year, but the film looks today irresistibly like a forecast about the new Germany of the 1930s. After the war, when a great deal of hunting took place, Robert Wise created the story again as a conscious parallel to the struggle with Nazism; called *A Game of Death* (1945), it featured John Loder, Audrey Long, and Jason Robards on the prowl. Still later, Akim Tamiroff took up the chase in *Black Forest* (1954), but the days of sportsmanship were evidently gone; when gunfights in the city are commonplace, who needs a desert island? In *Punishment Park* (1970), the most recent equivalent to the story, the prey stands no chance whatever.

Two minor excursions to the Island were *Terror is a Man* (1959), in which an attempt is made to transform a leopard into a man, and the Roger Corman production *Twilight People* (1971), directed by Eddie Romero and featuring an unrealistic attempt to create a super-race by turning people into animals – such hybrids including an Antelope Man and a Tree Woman, whose contributions to progress are difficult to measure. But the links here are with lycanthropy rather than with surgery; werewolves and vampires hover on the fringes of science fiction as if hoping for recognition by the Royal Society, and making occasional incursions in the form of Mowgli, racial leukaemia, and mental cases, but they remain inexplicable and insubstantial, illuminated by moonshine rather than by the harsh light of technical analysis.

The myth of the werewolf is nevertheless a potent one, perpetuated on film by the fascination of watching hair, teeth and claws sprout before one's eyes – living confirmation, as is Mr Hyde, that the mark of the beast is more than skin deep. The reverse process, after silver bullet or princess's kiss, is an equally traditional catharsis: slowly the frenzied lines die away like sins after Confession, and the mortal rests in peace or ascends to Heaven like Jean Marais in *La Belle et la Bête* (1948) clasping, in this instance, Josette Day, and uttering Cocteau's moral – 'Love can make a man a beast, but it can also turn ugliness to beauty'.

If the male is good wolf material, the female makes, it seems, a good cat. When RKO were looking for a sure-fire title in 1942 they found that *Cat People* got the best audience response, so they made a film to fit; it was the first production job of Val Lewton, whose eight years with RKO marked an output of haunting masterpieces, cheaply made but with a poetic terror in their use of shadows and superstitions. Directed by Jacques Tourneur, *Cat People* invented a Serbian legend that turned Simone Simon into a black panther at times of crisis; the transformation is not shown, and the film is the greater for it, the audience's imagination working overtime as the soundtrack rustles with ominous footsteps. The film was rather different from the implications of its title, but it made a brisk four million dollars; a sequel was inevitable. *The Curse of the Cat People* (1944), in which Robert Wise took a hand, featured Simone Simon's ghost but was otherwise many moons away from metamorphosis. It was Barbara Shelley in *Cat Girl* (1957) who came closest to the original by dreaming up a leopard to take revenge on her adulterous husband.

Unflatteringly, the ladies are also converted to snakes with some regularity. An early example was Rosemary Thebe, an Indian dancing girl in *The Reincarnation of Karma* (1912), made by the Vitagraph Company. The British followed suit with *The Vampire* (1913), *Heba the Snake Woman* (1915) and *The Beetle* (1919), and there has been much writhing and shedding of skin ever since, from Robert Siodmak's *Cobra Woman* (1944) to Andrew Meyer's *Night of the Cobra Woman* (1972), featuring Joy Bang in absent-minded disarray, but unfortunately failing to live up to Meyer's earlier promise as a maker of short films (his *Early Clue to the New Direction* is a fascinating Melvillean fantasy). Faith Domergue in *Cult of the Cobra* (1955) and Susan Travers in *The Snake Woman* (1960) should also be noted.

An unexpected classic in this area is *The Reptile* (1966), a Hammer production directed by John Gilling

as a companion piece to *Plague of the Zombies*, made in the same sets (at Bray) and at the same time. Sheltered by her father in a remote Cornish manor house, Jacqueline Pearce is the victim of an obscure Malayan sect; she periodically turns into a snake, sloughs her skin, and hibernates for the winter unless disturbed by intruders whom she promptly poisons with her fangs. The story is told with unusual dignity and control, concentrating on the Moreau-figure of the girl's father (Noel Willman), a proud but superstitious man incapable of rescuing his daughter from the fate half-wished upon her by himself. Reason finally triumphs over fear, and there is the inevitable exorcism by fire, but Gilling keeps it uncluttered for the most part and there are many wholly pleasing sequences – as when the snake-woman writhes on her bed to the crooning of the sinister Malay attendant, or when her father beats with frenzied disgust at the empty green skin still lying in its nightgown. Although only appearing as herself in two scenes (and all too rarely to be found on the cinema screen subsequently) Jacqueline Pearce quickly generates enough sympathy to ensure that her plight seems dis-

tressing even under the not-too-successful snake's head which bears an alarming resemblance to Marty Feldman. It's sad that Gilling hasn't been able to develop further along these lines in his later career.

Among Roger Corman's many aggressive heroines was Susan Cabot in *The Wasp Woman*, made at high speed along with half a dozen other films in 1959. A formidable career woman, she heads a giant cosmetics company that's doing badly because she's past her prime and no longer features in their publicity. One day a visitor demonstrates his rejuvenation drug, made from wasp wax and consequently stronger stuff than royal jelly; he injects a guinea-pig which shrinks promptly to what looks rather like a white mouse, and, much impressed, she enlists him to keep her looking young. It works for a while, until her innate waspishness takes over and she buzzes about with a black mask and wobbling antennae, sucking blood (a new departure for wasps but not, of course, for horror films). What acid does for her, it took a hydraulic press to accomplish for Al Hedison in Kurt Neumann's *The Fly* (1958), in which a prototype matter-transmitter gets its inventor's

Turning nasty: (left) Brett Halsey in *The Return of the Fly* (Fox, 1959); (right) Bruce Bennett in *The Alligator People* (Associated Producers Inc., 1959); and (right, below) Stewart Moss becomes one of *The Bat People* (AIP, 1972).

atoms mixed up with those of a bluebottle. Bristling with discomfort, the scientist is unable to disentangle his predicament, despite his multi-faceted view of the problem. Vincent Price played his brother, Patricia Owens his wife. The film was never as good as it should have been, although its final shot is much quoted: a fly with tiny human head and arm screams for help from a spider's web.

There was a predictable *Return of the Fly*, again with Vincent Price, the following year, but it was the third in the series, *The Curse of the Fly* (1965) which was the most distinguished of the trilogy. Directed by Don Sharp, it featured mental case Carole Gray breaking out from one asylum and marrying into another. Brian Donlevy has a bunch of monstrosities in his garden shed but gamely he plugs away in the cause of science to perfect his teleportation device, sending horrific mounds of tissue through the ether between London and Montreal. The plot is similarly encrusted with imperfections, including a malicious housekeeper trying to drive the mistress mad by playing the piano in the middle of the night, but the care with which Sharp concentrates on the unstable heroine, locked in images of imprisonment, hints usefully at deeper matters.

Cheerfully disregarding biological compatibilities, the cinema seems willing to change anybody into anything. In *The Alligator People* (1959), George Macready experimented with a serum derived from alligators. Working from the best possible motives, he reasoned that new limbs could thereby be grown on the disabled – but the disabled, with a fine logic, proceeded

to turn into alligators as a result, lurching disconsolately about the countryside with wrinkled chests, grinning teeth and baggy trousers. In 1966, the much-maligned Akim Tamiroff impersonated *The Vulture*, a 200-year old bird revitalized by nuclear transmutation; waving his feathers, he tears into Broderick Crawford but is plucked at the last moment from his attack on Diane Clare. And with *The Bat People* (1972), Stewart Moss gets bitten in a cave and is soon having fits of instant fur and frenzy; at the end, the bats adopt him and send for his wife to keep him company, which looks almost as daft as it sounds. Alan Arkin neatly scorned the whole menagerie in his *People Soup* (1969), a delightful short in which his two sons concoct a stew that turns one of them into a chicken and then a sheepdog.

It's said that communication with plants has already shown tentative indications of success, but horticultural experiments have so far been rare in the movies (with the respectful exception of *The Thing*, and *The Quatermass Experiment* which memorably integrated man and cactus). Roger Corman's quickest film, said to have been made in two days, features the cinema's single comedian-plant in *Little Shop of Horrors* (1960), for which screenplay writer Charles Griffith stole an idea or two from the H. G. Wells story *The Flowering of the Strange Orchid*. Growing at an alarming rate in Mushnick's Flower Shop, the unknown shrub finds a disciple in Dick Miller, an eccentric young man with a craving for carnations (which he munches on the spot, defending himself with a 'Don't knock it 'til you try it, huh?'). Acquiring a taste for blood, the plant devours everyone who comes near it, spitting out the bits it doesn't want and sending Miller out to get more. Finally consumed in his turn, he ends up as a coy bloom on one of its branches.

Donald Pleasence is the Moreau-figure in *The Mutation* (1972), insisting that plants and animals can be combined but apparently needing human flesh as a catalyst. His surgical failures are packed off to be exhibited at a freak show, but one of them, a former student turned Venus fly-trap, escapes to rescue Julie Ege who is already stretched in the approximate nude (her stand-in reveals more than Miss Ege herself) beneath the surgeon's knife. The evil genius and his monstrous offspring are consumed in a laboratory fire, while the girl goes into a grateful clinch with her nearest boy-friend, the leaves already beginning to grow along her arm. The film was directed in a dispirited manner by Jack Cardiff, and it makes one long not only for his better days but for the return of the Jack Arnold era, when even the perambulating crystalline rocks of *The Monolith Monsters* (1957), directed by John Sherwood from an Arnold script, had a dark and majestic splendour. Converting all in their path to instant statues, these towering growths rumble across the desert under the influence of an alien germ, infesting the landscape like skyscrapers. Until, perhaps, somebody has a shot at filming J. G. Ballard's novel *Crystal World*, we shall not see their kind again.

The matter of size, as we've noted with films like *Incredible Shrinking Man*, is an important element in science fiction. The literature itself is based on different perspectives, fresh methods of examining problems that were being taken too much for granted; it distorts the conventional in order to reassess it. The technique is simple but effective – a slight change in the dimensions of anything familiar causes disorientation and alarm, whether it be a book that won't quite fit on the shelf or a door that jams in hot weather. We live by a set of unconscious relativities matched to average human standards but in any other respects quite arbitrary, and film, which itself distorts normal laws of size and time, is in a unique position to challenge them – if for no other purpose than to shake us up a little.

It is admittedly unlikely that the Shrinking Man's discovery that a pair of scissors is too huge for him to lift will be an experience his audience can ever share for themselves, but as a crisis it is potent enough for us to identify with him. Fears of objects too vast to control have both a physical and an instinctual origin, linked with our fears of things as they *are*: an insect can assume a remarkable range of sizes according to whether you loathe it, like it, or couldn't care less. And the experience of seeing the thing on the cinema screen is utterly different from that of spraying it off the roses.

Movie monsters, then, have a complexity of appeal in which sympathy, responsibility, repugnance and fear, plus a shaking of the confidence in what's 'normal' and what isn't, can compel our fascinated attention. The cinema's greatest example is *King Kong* (1933), chiefly because he was the most convincing, despite the rippling fur and the sometimes hesitant movements, and because he was a giant. There had been many apes before him, including *Balaoo the Demon Baboon* (1913); *The Gorilla* (made in both 1927 and 1930, with Walter Pidgeon in both versions of Ralph Spence's play); *The Monster Walks* (1932), and at least two versions of *Murders in the Rue Morgue* (1914 and 1931), in which the innocent villain of the piece is an ape (directed in 1931 by Bela Lugosi to bring back victims for his research into blood transfusions). There were even humanoid apes, like Bull Montana in *Go and Get It* (1920) impersonating a monkey with a murderer's brain, or Lon Chaney in *A Blind Bargain* (1922), the deformed result of monkey gland grafts, or George Kotsonaros in *The Wizard* (1927), a man-faced ape with shining scalp, heavy brow, and fur sprouting abruptly at collar-level. The ground had been extensively covered by the time *Island of Lost Souls* came into view in 1932, and there seemed no reason why the arrival of *Kong* in the following year should cause the sensation it did. Yet it was the only film ever to appear simultaneously at the world's two largest theatres, the Roxy and the Radio City Music Hall, and, like Frankenstein, Kong has been around ever since.

The triumph was that of Willis O'Brien, the master of simian special effects who had been giving life to prehistoric scenes since 1915 (his first film was *The Dinosaur and the Missing Link*, which got him a job with the Edison Company in New York). But it was also a triumph for Merian C. Cooper, flying ace turned film-maker, who had been called in to rescue RKO from bankruptcy, and for five years had wanted to set up a gorilla picture featuring the giant dragon lizards of

Walter Pidgeon goes ape with Alice Day in the silent version of *The Gorilla* (First National, 1927).

(below) A Willis O'Brien Brachiosaurus casts an eye over Bessie Love in *The Lost World* (First National, 1927). (opposite) Two scenes from Robert Fuest's *The Final Programme* (Anglo-EMI, 1974), with Jon Finch as Jerry Cornelius and Sarah Douglas as his murdered sister Catherine.

Komodo. It was even a small triumph for Edgar Wallace, who had worked with Cooper on an early script for the film but died in 1932 before anything was completed; to this day his name remains associated with the finished production.

Most of all, it was a triumph for two eighteen-inch steel skeletons coated with latex rubber and rabbit pelts, issuing sounds derived from lowering a lion's roar one octave and re-recording it backwards. Together with an assortment of full-size limbs and matte (composite) shots, they comprised the giant gorilla who is discovered on a remote island (the same jungle sets were used as in *Most Dangerous Game*, made at the same time; Leslie Banks stalked them by day, Kong by night). The gorilla is brought to New York, and shot down from the Empire State Building after trampling the city in search of Fay Wray. Kong is violent, ruthless and dangerous, crushing and dismembering humans with casual brutality. But the aircraft that make the final lethal attack are seen from the target's viewpoint, firing their guns directly out at the audience. When Kong falls, we all fall. Many forces are symbolized by his huge, amiable figure, but the most vital is his innocence. As long as technology, capitalism, or mere insensitivity are seeking to enslave us, Kong will be there to break the chains.

Or, to put it another way, the release of unthinking forces brings chaos. The monster ape, snarling menace over the roof-tops, is as handy a symbol for Hitler as for liberty. And he gets toppled from his perch at the end. Whichever way you look at him, he's satisfying – and

such fun for the kids. Better than the Komodo dragon lizards he had first wanted, Cooper included O'Brien's dinosaurs in the film; they too answered a perpetual public need, even if some had to be cut out for reasons of length. And although the fight between Kong and a pterodactyl is surprisingly easy to forget – it's Kong who dominates all recollection of the film – the lumbering monsters still confirmed for all time that the cinema without its prehistoric reptiles and its variations on the Beauty and the Beast fairy-tale would·be unthinkable.

When Sir Arthur Conan Doyle visited the United States in June 1922, he brought with him a film which, rough and untitled as it was, hinted at a startling authenticity. Perhaps, after all, *The Lost World* was based on fact? The *New York Times* announced with excitement: 'His monsters of the ancient world or of the new world which he has discovered in the ether, were extraordinarily lifelike. If fakes, they were masterpieces.' Conan Doyle revealed the following day that the film had been created by Willis O'Brien as a sequence for *The Lost World*, the logical next step for the animator after his *Ghost of Slumber Mountain* (1919) in which a magic telescope revealed life in prehistoric times, including a tyrannosaurus and a triceratops in terrifying combat. Conan Doyle's support meant that the production of *The Lost World* could go ahead, and despite the unremarkable human performances it was a huge hit when it was released in 1925, obtaining also the distinction of being the first in-flight film when it was shown over Berlin in February 1926 by the German Air Service Company.

Any parent will know of the grip of the dinosaur on the imagination of the young. The island of time which has somehow avoided change and discovery continues to be hotly debated as a geographical possibility in the nurseries and playrooms of the world, and dinosaurs are knowledgeably identified whether in cartoon or tabletop-model form. Kong may have his progeny (*Son of Kong*, 1933; *White Pongo*, 1945; *Mighty Joe Young*, 1949; *King Kong Escapes*, 1967), but even more frequent are the revelations that dinosaurs continue to trundle and snarl in an obscure valley or distant plateau. Willis O'Brien, although frequently ignored and overlooked as the originator of the technique that made the monsters possible, was able to contribute a prehistoric sequence to Irwin Allen's *The Animal World* (1956) and created the radioactive paleosaurus on a tiny budget for *The Giant Behemoth* (1959); but he was excluded from King Kong's encounter with Godzilla in Japan in 1962, and employed but unused for the remake of *The Lost World* in 1960, which committed the indignity of plastering fake fins on alligators and iguanas. His 1941 designs for *Gwangi* were closely followed for *The Valley of Gwangi*, the title under which the story was finally made in 1968, but were uncredited. Ray Harryhausen, however, who was O'Brien's protégé, has had better luck, and with the effect he calls

Dynamation has outshone all competition – although the monsters by Karel Zeman in *Journey to the Beginning of Time* (1954), and those of Roger Dicken for *The Land that Time Forgot* (1974), run him close. Changing to Dynarama for *The Golden Voyage of Sinbad* (1973), Harryhausen presented such spectacular fantasies as a flying demon, a one-eyed centaur, and a six-armed, sabre-swinging statue come to life.

In the tradition of Conan Doyle, dinosaurs wandered (in a green-tinted sequence, preserved by uranium deposits) on *The Lost Continent* (1951), but were replaced by giant crabs and jellyfish when the title cropped up again in 1968, adapted this time from Dennis Wheatley's *Uncharted Seas*. Virgil Vogel's *The Land Unknown* (1957) uncovered a tropical oasis in the Antarctic, complete with dinosaurs and man-eating plants. In the previous year, *The Mole People* (1956) had

Making advances. (above) Cynthia Patrick in the clutches of *The Mole People* (Universal, 1956); (left) the poisonous dragon in *Reptilicus* (Saga, 1961); (below) an early victim of the invisible shrieking dinosaur in *The Prehistoric Sound* (Zurbano, 1964). (opposite, above) Giant scorpion meets giant whelk among the carnivorous seaweeds of *The Lost Continent* (Hammer, 1968). (opposite below) Lynne Frederick is rescued from the ants in *Phase IV* (Paramount, 1973).

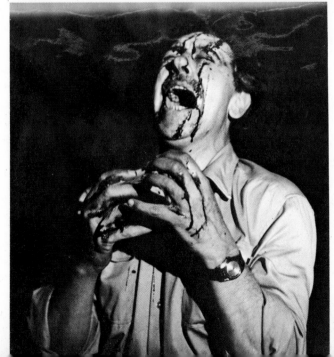

found Vogel underground in Sumeria, unearthing a tribe of albinos and their mole-like slaves; he had an infectious enthusiasm for the outlandish. And if the cost of travel was too high for the production budget, the dinosaur could always obligingly raise its head on the studio's doorstep, like *Reptilicus* (1962), dug up piecemeal from a Danish bog and reconstituting itself into a poisonous dragon with impenetrable scales.

For the ultimate in economy, the creature could even be invisible, as in *The Prehistoric Sound* (1964), cheaply made on the Bronston lot in Madrid by José Nieves-Condé, with photography by Manuel Berenguer (second-unit cameraman on such films as *Dr Zhivago*). Disdaining plausibility, the plot for this one centres on an invisible prehistoric monster inadvertently hatched out by treasure-hunters in the Greek mountains. Identifiable by its thudding foot-falls, its hideous shrieks when aroused, and its habit of ripping humans to pieces, the invisible menace lays siege to a nearby house in which its discoverers take refuge, and manages bloodily to dispose of several of them before being burned (and briefly glimpsed – a wobbling lizard) on the roof of a jeep. A modest enough item, with Ingrid Pitt turning up surprisingly in its cast, the film displays an unabashed dexterity in its action sequences, in which there is much dashing at full belt across the countryside.

One of the vintage years for science-fiction films was 1953, the year of *War of the Worlds*, *Invaders from Mars*, *Donovan's Brain*, *Them!*, and the two Bradbury-derived classics *It Came from Outer Space* and *The Beast from 20,000 Fathoms*. Related somewhat remotely to Bradbury's melancholy story *The Fog Horn*, Eugène Lourié's *Beast* featured a rhedosaurus, melted from the Arctic ice by atomic tests, making its way to New York

(its former breeding ground) and being demolished at last in an amusement park on Manhattan Beach. The film made a brisk profit in excess of five million dollars, confirming once again the convincing nature of Ray Harryhausen's special effects, seen at their best in the final scenes. Other aquatic visitors followed in its wake, with *Monster from the Ocean Floor* (1954) and *It Came from Beneath the Sea* (1955), but the most illustrious was also in production in 1953 – *The Creature from the Black Lagoon*. A genetic compendium to delight the heart of Moreau, the Gill Man lurks like a sullen demon to reach from the depths for unsuspecting girls, an expression of dark sexuality filmed by Jack Arnold in brooding patterns of light and shadow. The Creature was back for its *Revenge* in 1955, and *Walked Among Us* (under the direction of John Sherwood) in 1956. In 1963, it went to Russia, where *The Amphibious Man* followed

(below) *Revenge of the Creature* (Universal, 1955).
(right) John Agar and Julie Adams tackle the Gill Man in *The Creature from the Black Lagoon* (Universal, 1954).

Arnold's example in its lyrical underwater choreography but made explicit the romantic implications of the Marine Devil's hunt for a girl.

Japanese saurians are, of course, in a class of their own, bred in vast numbers by Ishiro Honda in the reasonable expectation that several lovable monsters are likely to be several times more popular than one. It all began with *Godzilla* (1955), a fire-breathing dinosaur that became a national hero; he was quickly given an entourage of charmingly unlikely associates, mostly radioactive and inclined to crush Tokyo at least once a year as if to provide masochistic reminders of past horrors. Battling with everything from *The Thing* (1964) to the *Smog Monster* (1971), Godzilla had a grand reunion in *Destroy All Monsters* (1968), in which the entire menagerie was sent out to crush the cities of the world under the guid-

adapted by Philip Yordan from the Carl Stephenson story *Leiningen versus the Ants*, it tells how Charlton Heston, stuck in the Amazon, advertises for a wife via his brother back home, and gets Eleanor Parker, gorgeous in white and eager to please. 'Frankly, Madam,' he observes, cracking nuts with one fist, 'you're not what I expected.' It appears, however, that she can play the piano, which mellows the mood until she reveals she has been married before; he asserts, with curling lip, that he's too proud to take someone else's leavings, and she responds spiritedly that if he knew anything about music he'd know that a piano is better for having been played. The arrival of the driver ants ('a monster forty miles square') puts a stop to the wisecracks; the lady stands by her man while the natives panic and run, and with his plantation about to

ance of villainous aliens, directing events from a flying saucer and keeping their own monster, Ghidorah, in reserve. Mount Fuji provided the setting for the final struggle, the human participants were, as usual, inconsequential, and there was no hope whatever that the film's title would mean the end of an era.

In 1953, it was also the time of the ant, with Byron Haskin's *The Naked Jungle* being followed by Gordon Douglas's *Them!*, usually the better remembered of the two. Resplendent with Paramount production values, *The Naked Jungle* is in fact well worth a second look;

be consumed he gets to thinking about alternatives. 'Tell me about women,' he suggests. 'It's a subject I find interesting.'

As in *War of the Worlds*, love arrives just in time to avert the disaster, and as in that earlier Haskin film there is some assistance from natural forces – in this case a dynamited dam causes a flood that washes the ants away from a landscape that looks as though the Martians have been at it. The scenes of Heston battling his way through the milling swarms of ants are quite horrific; actually they were wood ants, and he had to be bathed in syrup to get them anywhere near him, but the film's previous scenes of screaming ant victims are convincing enough for one to believe that he'll be reduced to a skeleton in ten seconds. Beautifully shot in colour by Ernest Laszlo, *Naked Jungle* is presented with style and elegance, and like *War of the Worlds* it contains the wistful certainty that the time for such qualities has already slipped away.

The marauding ants in *Naked Jungle*, advancing across an appalling desert, are matched by the monsters in *Them!*, emerging through mists of sand after an atomic blast has expanded them to giants. Slowly the news filters through to the nearest towns that the desert contains a more substantial menace than noises made by a 'freakish' wind, and James Whitmore investigates, his eyes like an insect's beneath curving goggles. Rather than an 'atomic' movie, the film is about the struggle between humans and the elements unleashed by the planet on which they attempt to live, elements which invade their cities and prove their vulnerability. Just as the Gill Man can only be driven back when he has been isolated far from his natural element, the ants are omnipotent in their own territory and none too easy to destroy outside it.

Extracts from both *Them!* and *Naked Jungle* were used in Walon Green's *The Hellstrom Chronicle* (1971) to show, nearly twenty years later, that the battle was still in progress, indeed that it has intensified. The film is a glowing documentary, crammed with extraordinary close-ups of the creatures that surround us daily (more or less), poised for the kill. Bristling with admonition, *Hellstrom Chronicle* makes an insistent assault on our complacency in the person of the fictional entomologist Nils Hellstrom (Lawrence Pressman) who, haggard and intense, addresses us interminably from rooftops, jungles, laboratories, observatories and his own back yard. 'Learn the inevitable destiny of ignorance,' he invites, with apparent glee at the imminent disappearance of mankind beneath a heaving mound of insects, and then proceeds to dazzle us with quantities of inconclusive, sometimes even misleading material (the remark that spiders are 'close relatives of the insect' seems particularly unhelpful). Hellstrom's low opinion of his species is given an extra charge by the ambiguous theological references that seem to be a necessary part of every screen scientist's vocabulary; on the one hand, 'man is unable to accept, as the insects do, that the purpose of life is life itself', on the other 'if man does have a relationship with God, it's because he alone can undo God's work' (this last, after Hellstrom has spread chaos among the insect life of his garden with a high-velocity hose).

The film's muddled sensationalism seems doubly unfortunate: firstly because the statistics *are* impressive if allowed to speak for themselves – insects *can* survive nuclear explosions, pull objects 100 times their own weight, lay 86,400 eggs a day, get through 80,000 tons

of foliage at a single infestation; secondly because the brilliant photographic accomplishments of the film's five cameramen reveal the actualities of everyday insect existence with a vividness, clarity and beauty which excel anything previously done in insect research. The film is a fascinating succession of brutal, eery visions of the battleground passing unnoticed beneath our feet; as a reptile sinks quivering beneath a flood of driver ants, it's impossible to watch this real-life restaging of *Them!* without a growing itch of disquiet.

The ants returned in Saul Bass's *Phase IV* (1973), the first feature film of the designer made famous by his credit titles, his work for Hitchcock, and his delightful short *Why Man Creates*. Written by Mayo Simon and turned subsequently into the book-of-the-film by

(opposite) A sample of Japanese promotion with *Son of Godzilla* (Toho, 1966).
(below) Charlton Heston gets the itch in *The Naked Jungle* (Paramount, 1953).

Barry Malzberg, *Phase IV* tells how all the ants in the Arizona desert team up against Nigel Davenport, foil each of his attempts to destroy them and finally manage to recruit him to support their cause. Although impeded by histrionics, the film is magnificently designed, with spectacular ant photography by Ken Middleham. There are moments of horror worthy of Bunuel, such as the ants emerging from a hole in a dead man's hand, and the conclusion suggests that our defences are genuinely beginning to crumble before an enemy that has learned to know us too well. The genetic intermingling implied by such exploits as *Wasp Woman* can be forgotten; if the ants develop a master-mind, the size of the creature will bear no relation whatever to the size of the problem he'll cause.

Poised for the kill: (right) An ant inspects Lynne Frederick in Saul Bass's *Phase IV* (Paramount, 1973); (below) Craig Stevens demonstrates the unlikely dimensions of *The Deadly Mantis* (Universal, 1957); (below right) Leo G. Carroll studies the growth rate of his *Tarantula* (Universal, 1955).

It has been a long and occasionally ludicrous fight, featuring many a tottering nightmare. There was the famous *Tarantula!* (1955) and the infamous *Earth versus the Spider* (1958). There was the *Deadly Mantis* (1957), *The Black Scorpion* (1957), and an *Attack of the Giant Leeches* (1959). Wasps were on the warpath in *Monster from Green Hell* (1956), snails in René Laloux's *Les Escargots* (1965), while Frank Finlay unleashed *The Deadly Bees* (1966) to kill anyone coated in his special 'essence of fear'. On one Island, the *Killer Shrews* (1959) were grown to the size of greyhounds, and on the *Island of the Doomed* (1966) a new Moreau experimented with a blood-sucking tree. Back on the mainland, Stuart Whitman and Janet Leigh endured *The Night of the Lepus* (1972), a humourless adaptation from Russell Braddon's *The Year of the Angry Rabbit*, made with one

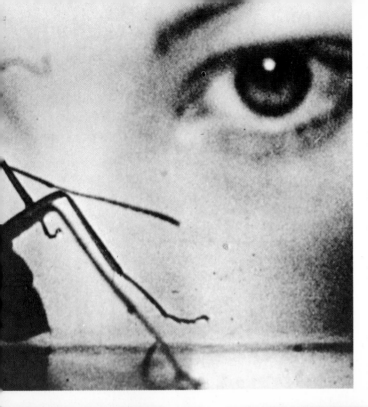

eye on *Them!* and featuring some stock-shots from *War of the Worlds* and a tolerably unpleasant concluding scene of carnage. The problem was that rabbits, even with false teeth splashed with red, don't look even slightly dangerous, and the film was unable to make them convincingly gigantic despite its slow-motion and scaled-down sets. Rather more successful are the rats of *Willard* (1970) and its successor *Ben* (1972), not in suggesting menace but in being themselves and causing exaggerated concern to such as Elsa Lanchester and Ernest Borgnine. Presented with loving care and expense, they come across as a tidy and self-possessed species, clearly better equipped psychologically than the humans who fall screaming beneath their disinterested feet. They make an excellent case for being permitted to take over.

In a remarkable début, George McCowan directed one of the best ecological revenge films in *Frogs* (1972), in which Ray Milland snarls and grumbles in his Southern mansion while the occupants of the surrounding swamplands mass for unexplained attack. To the

accompaniment of a gradual crescendo of croaks and rustles, the reptilian army, which includes spiders, leeches, turtles and salamanders, picks off the members of the household until Milland remains alone waiting for the blanket of lethal bodies to fall upon him. Once again, the days when Nature could be ludicrously caricatured by something like *The Giant Claw* (1957), a pop-eyed and scraggy ball of feathers on a wire, have been chillingly consigned to oblivion.

Defeat is also the fate of humanity in *Chosen Survivors* (1973), a modest but attractively mounted melodrama in which visitors to a survival centre deep underground find themselves trapped there by the outbreak of nuclear war up above. The customary tensions and liaisons are quickly set up as they attempt to adjust to

their predicament, and the already wavering balance is completely disrupted when they find that the only other survivors of the holocaust are clouds of vampire bats who find their way into the corridors from a nearby cavern. These conveniently black shapes (the process shots are wholly convincing), uttering amplified screams, descend abruptly round the heads of the humans in a struggle made the more sinister by dim single-colour lighting. An obvious derivation from *The Birds*, these scenes of panic save the script from having to consider too deeply the implications of its opening, and the ending is sheer cop-out, but as another skirmish with evolution it leaves a scar or two. The trend continues with such films as *Bug* (1975) and *Jaws* (1975).

High above them all is *The Birds* itself, created by

Hitchcock in 1963 with barely a nod to Daphne du Maurier who wrote the original story. At first sight a seemingly weak, anticlimactic venture, and so reduced by the small screen as to be worth avoiding when repeated on television, *The Birds* reveals itself on the cinema screen as the most accurate and terrifying attack on our illusions since the shower-bath murder in *Psycho*. Chiefly one notices the assault by the soundtrack, Bernard Herrmann's superb orchestration of electronic effects by Remi Gassman and Oskar Sala, a harsh, unearthly tirade that batters our ears as the plunging gulls and crows hurl themselves at our eyes. And one notices, of course, the process shots, sometimes awkward, sometimes obscure, sometimes too crowded to identify. Whether you believe them or not – and under the pressure of sound and panic it's difficult not to – they are so brilliantly mixed with shots you *have* to believe (the crows waiting by the school, the whirring cloud that comes out of the fireplace, the snapping beak that tears a frantic hand) that the power remains intact.

But where, comes the repeated question, do the birds come from? Why do they attack? Hitchcock covers all the explanations in his trailer (revenge for our centuries-old exploitation of them), and primarily in the scene at the Bodega Bay restaurant: it's the end of the world, or a freakish result of atmospheric conditions, or an attack brought on by the presence of outsider Melanie Daniels (Tippi Hedren). We are given all the choices, and at the same time we are given no reason to accept any of them – the birds, as birds, are inexplicable. Their function is surely to externalize the chaotic insecurity we make for ourselves and which is made for us; their threat is that of anything beyond our control, be it geographical, political, mental or metaphysical. And their effect is to draw us closer together, to share a common humanity. It's a poor enough protection, but it might keep the wolf from the door a little longer.

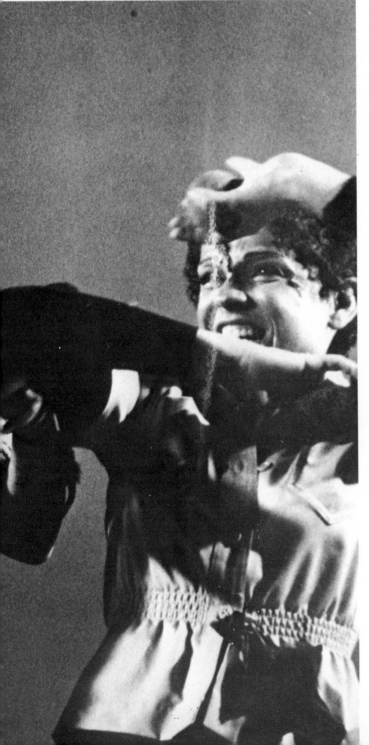

The scars of defeat. (above) Rod Taylor dodges a crow in Hitchcock's *The Birds* (Universal, 1963), while (left) scores of vampire bats descend upon the *Chosen Survivors* (Columbia-Warner, 1974).

ARMAGEDDON

But what were we to begin to do in that graveyard of a world? Could ever men have been faced with such a question since the dawn of time? It is true that our own physical needs, and even our luxuries, were assured for the future. All the stores of food, all the vintages of wine, all the treasures of art were ours for the taking. But what were we to do? Edward D. Malone.

AND LATER

Harry Belafonte roams the streets of New York in *The World, the Flesh, and the Devil* (MGM, 1959).

As part of the process of building a new world, science-fiction writers often find it convenient to dispose of the old one. A wide choice of catastrophes is offered, ranging from Velikovsky's unstable solar system (which serves to explain not only the Red Spot on Jupiter but also much of the Old Testament) to the return of the ice age in John Christopher's *World in Winter*. Poison gases in space, radioactive meteorites, comets from nowhere, solar instability, even the super-saturation of matter, have been used in science fiction to set chaos in motion and examine the consequences, while among the less 'natural' causes are such favourites as plagues, the results of experiments run wild, the master plans of mad scientists, ecological breakdown, and of course nuclear warfare. The planet is in fact so precariously situated, politically, volcanically, spatially or whatever, that its survival would appear to depend on the miraculous, not to mention the unreasonable.

That the end of the world makes such an attractive theme can be attributed to rather more than alarmism, although the activities of Bible-thumpers have made an inevitable contribution. The landscapes of disaster carry a powerful symbolic charge, representing not only the

summation of former mistakes but also the prospects for rebuilding; the challenge of ruins is such that they are seldom neglected for long. More subjectively the disappearance of millions of one's fellow-men, leaving the advantage of their accomplishments unencumbered by the disadvantages of their presence, offers a remedy to many a modest paranoia. Free access to an unlimited supply of luxuries in a context where the only law is one's own – the situation has a utopian ring to it, and it blends seductively with a philosophy that is equal parts of Rousseau and Heinlein, stating that man lives best from his own resources of courage, energy and industry. Above all, Armageddon *simplifies*: questions of morality and responsibility may legitimately be set aside in favour of basic matters like survival and the perpetuation of the species. Inner strengths are confirmed by external emergencies.

In *Things to Come* (1936) the social collapse and its consequences are clearly defined. When World War II ends in 1966, and inflation has reached heights that seem almost plausible for the 1970s (the price of a newspaper is £4·00), Everytown is a ragged heap of architectural and human relics. Afflicted with 'Wandering Sickness',

its inhabitants stagger despondently in preparation for continued fighting, headed by a ruthless warlord, the Chief (Ralph Richardson), who revels in personal wealth and power. It has become a familiar community in science fiction, repeated particularly in the novels of John Wyndham and John Christopher, but also taken up by American writers, to whom gun-toting provincial dictators come as less of a shock. But where Heinlein can regard the autocrat as a hero (in *Farnham's Freehold*, for example), Wells sees *his* Chief as a degenerate anachronism, and short-circuits history by having the future arrive in the form of Raymond Massey to impose progress through technology. The Chief is killed by an overdose of peace gas, and Massey takes over the fortunes of the world; he's just another dictator, but you can tell he's also a gentleman, so it doesn't matter.

Although the Chief was the first of his kind in the cinema, the images of ruin were a familiar backcloth, not least because of their resemblance to documentaries of World War I. The world had ended on a number of occasions already on the screen, beginning with the Kalem fantasy *The Comet* (1910), which burned the planet to a desert and set the trend for pre-atomic

Burning with impatience. (left) The colonists prepare to leave in *When Worlds Collide* (Paramount, 1951), while (below) Edward Judd and Janet Munro prepare to stay for *The Day the Earth Caught Fire* (British Lion, 1961).

disasters. In 1916, there was a *Comet's Comeback*, slowing down the Earth's rotation with poison gases, and in the same year Nordisk brought about the *End of the World*. Directed by August Blom, this was an elaborate production in which the approaching comet inspires orgiastic excesses on the part of the rich, and vengeful muttering on the part of the poor. As fireballs rain down, the two classes confront each other in a startling outbreak of gunfire, but the heroine is carried to safety across what appear to be genuine floods and she rings a church bell until her lover appears. Superbly photographed, the final sequences are a great improvement on the catastrophe itself, which consists largely of sparklers bouncing across a table-top model of a village; but the Adam-and-Eve ending is less interesting than the earlier convolutions of the plot, which embraces a laboratory power-struggle, an industrial riot, and a remarkably inept bit of choreography by a simpering *danseuse*.

In France, the Eiffel Tower was a refuge in *Paris Qui Dort* and a casualty in *La Cité Foudroyée*, both made in 1923 and both featuring wildly misapplied ray-guns; but the Mary Pickford film *Waking Up the Town* (1925) restored the cometary collision theme (although mostly for laughs) and by 1930 Abel Gance was using a comet for his *La Fin du Monde*. Like most Gance films, it took a while to complete, and the English version was not circulated until 1934, doubtless with some influence on Wells and Korda. They may well also have seen *Deluge* (1933), which derived from the spectacular flooding sequences of Michael Curtiz's *Noah's Ark* (1929), and which in turn provided a source for the special effects in *SOS Tidal Wave* (1938) and a large number of later serials whenever they called for the drowning of New York.

They would certainly have *read* Philip Wylie's *When Worlds Collide*, published in 1932 and written

83

in partnership with Edwin Balmer (as was its sequel, *After Worlds Collide*, which appeared in 1934), but the late '30s and the '40s were evidently cataclysmic enough, while the concept of the atomic bomb made comets appear almost trivial. It was not until 1951 that, on the strength of his success with *Destination Moon*, George Pal resurrected the story and created the definitive interplanetary disaster film, influenced no doubt by the fact that Cecil B. De Mille had originally planned to make it in 1934 and would characteristically have spared no expense. Directed by Rudolph Maté (the man who photographed Dreyer's classic *Joan of Arc*), and brilliantly designed by space-artist Chesley Bonestell, the film describes how a dying Sun enters the solar system on a collision course with Earth, allowing eight months for a spaceship to be constructed that will take a handful of survivors to a new planet that has arrived at the same time. The disintegration of society under this pressure is a rather decorous affair (one of the worst excesses involves using banknotes to light a cigarette), but the final sequences, bathed in Technicolor orange, are classics of destruction only matched, thirty years later, by the special effects in *Earthquake*, one of a new series of disaster epics. Few other comets have made any impression (even a real one, Kohoutek, was anticlimactic); usually they are to be found standing in for the Bomb – as with Max De Haas's *Dream Without End* (1964), a melancholy short film telling how news of a comet on collision course finds most of the world too involved in its own affairs to give a damn.

Such natural disasters as followed *When Worlds Collide* dealt firmly in terms of man having brought it upon himself, rather than hinting that the Heavens had lost patience. Bomb tests knock the Earth off its axis in Val Guest's *Day the Earth Caught Fire* (1961), and Edward Judd and Janet Munro get hot and bothered in the resultant heatwave; the film is slickly made, in a tone of petulant frustration which accurately captures the mood of the British press at the time – not surprisingly in that it starred the *Daily Express* and its former editor, Arthur Christiansen. In 1965, *Crack in the World* had Dana Andrews firing a missile at the earth's core, setting off a string of earthquakes along the Macedo Fault, and trying to put things right by loosing off a nuclear bomb inside a volcano. Through red apocalyptic filters, he creates a new moon when a great wedge of the earth is flung into space.

But these were mere diversions compared with the real issue at hand. Closer to the point were Robert Aldrich's *Kiss Me Deadly* (1955) and Tadeusz Konwicki's *Last Day of Summer* (1957), or, sandwiched between them, Peter Foldes's *Short Vision*; these were films of anxiety and pain whose protagonists wandered in the shadow of imminent, searing ruin. Taken from a Mickey Spillane original, the Aldrich film is the most memorable, with Ralph Meeker as the archetypal

Mike Hammer on the trail of 'the mysterious They who'll even kill for the sake of the Great Whatsit'. They turns out to be a contemporary Pandora, flinging wide the magic box to let loose a mushroom cloud. In *Short Vision*, the Whatsit is a flying saucer, hovering at night over a forest and exploding abruptly to melt the flesh from every living thing below. Foldes's animation, characteristically preoccupied with metamorphosis, captures the nightmare of collapsing faces and shrivelling bodies in merciless detail. In *Last Day of Summer*, a man and a woman sit on a beach, remembering one war and anticipating another, as jet planes scream overhead; it's a *Marienbad* situation – they might have met before – but the uncertainties have a nuclear inference, and they lie on the sand like derelicts before allowing themselves to be washed away by the sea. Ten years later, when Michael Cacoyannis dumped Pandora's box on the island of Karos in the Aegean, *The Day the Fish Came Out* demonstrated that the theme gained

nothing from overstatement, despite the attraction of having Candice Bergen dance 'The Jet' while radio-activity poisons the water supply.

The Bomb was falling on the screen as early as 1951 (or even 1946, if we admit Lionel Atwill's inauguration of World War III in *Lost City in the Jungle*, or Norman Taurog's Government-approved explanation of Hiroshima, *The Beginning or the End*). It was with Arch Oboler's *Five* (1951), however, that the wave of nuclear films properly began, reaching its height in the early 1960s; disturbingly, Oboler already had no difficulty in presenting his story in an entirely post-atomic context, or his audience in accepting this grisly 'first', in which the United States are inherited by a Negro, a cashier, a mountaineer, an idealist and a pregnant girl. In an elegant cliff-top mansion, they wrangle and fight in continuation of the prejudices and insanities that put them there; the girl drags them in search of her husband through a nearby city strewn with corpses, but at last settles for a substitute. Reflecting Oboler's background in radio, *Five* was full of talk and vociferous warning, although visually it lacked subtlety; it was quickly followed by Alfred Green's *Invasion USA* (1952), which reversed the formula. Soviet

(below and bottom left) Scenes from Andrew Marton's *Crack in the World* (Paramount, 1965), in which a nuclear device is lowered into a volcano.

(right) Gaby Rodgers opens the box in Robert Aldrich's *Kiss Me Deadly* (United Artists, 1955) and is instantly destroyed by the unleashed radioactivity. Superbly photographed by Ernest Laszlo, this is one of the great films of nuclear paranoia.

missiles plunge on America, watched on television by a horrified group of bar-room drinkers, each of whom is killed as he attempts to leave for home. The whole thing turns out to be the result of the hypnotic powers of one of the barflies (played by Dan O'Herlihy) and is intended to persuade us to prepare for trouble, but it's disturbing enough while it lasts. By 1960, when rockets tumbled yet again on Manhattan in *Rocket Attack USA*, the possibility that it might only be fantasy had long been discarded – such reassurances no longer made any impression.

The cinema's loudest warning came in the form of *On the Beach* (1959), derived from Nevil Shute's best-seller and premiered in 18 cities simultaneously around the world (with a special full-page advertisement in *The Times*). Produced and directed by Stanley Kramer, starring Gregory Peck, Ava Gardner, Fred Astaire and Anthony Perkins, it was photographed by Giuseppe Rotunno (Visconti's brilliant cameraman), and clearly had no intention of being overlooked. It showed a bleak picture of a world dying from the effects of nuclear warfare, with radiation sweeping down to wipe out the last survivors in Australia, where suicide pills have already been issued. Spasmodic radio

(right) Peter Foldes' artwork for *A Short Vision* (1956). (below) Ava Gardner watches the submarine begin its final journey in *On the Beach* (United Artists, 1959).

(opposite above) Charlton Heston with plague victim in *The Omega Man* (Warners, 1971). (opposite below) Cornel Wilde's marauders on the attack in *No Blade of Grass* (MGM, 1970).

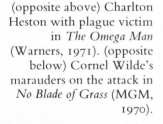

signals tempt Gregory Peck's submarine back for an inspection of San Francisco, but the hope that, after all, some Americans have survived, proves groundless, and the city's streets are chillingly deserted. Back in Melbourne, Fred Astaire takes part in the world's last motor race, an event in which the drivers have no need to care whether they live or die, while Perkins and wife wonder how long to postpone giving the pill to their first-born, and Peck and Gardner ripple their jaw-muscles at the futility of it all. The film is achingly sincere yet curiously resistible; it has an air of immaculate calm, as though nothing unusual were happening, and although one could argue that this would be precisely the effect of global catastrophe, the ugly explosions of anarchy that have been described by, for example, Rudolph Wurlitzer (*Quake*) or Peter van Greenaway (*The Crucified City*), read more plausibly.

Kramer may have appeared to have had the last word, but *On the Beach* was in fact only a halfway point, poised between the raw gloom of the '50s and the desperation of the '60s, when for a while it looked as though all the warnings had been in vain. Where *On the Beach* concentrated on why it shouldn't happen, *Dr Strangelove* and *Fail Safe* showed exactly how it could, given the nature of the world's security system. Both films demonstrated with giant screens the routine flights of nuclear bombers on the Soviet border and showed how easily a human or mechanical fault could edge them into attack. Both films showed the American and Russian Presidents collaborating to recall or destroy the bombers after they have been unleashed. And in both films, all attempts fail. The world's auto-

(pages 88–89) The drowning of New York, spectacularly performed in *When Worlds Collide* (Paramount, 1951).

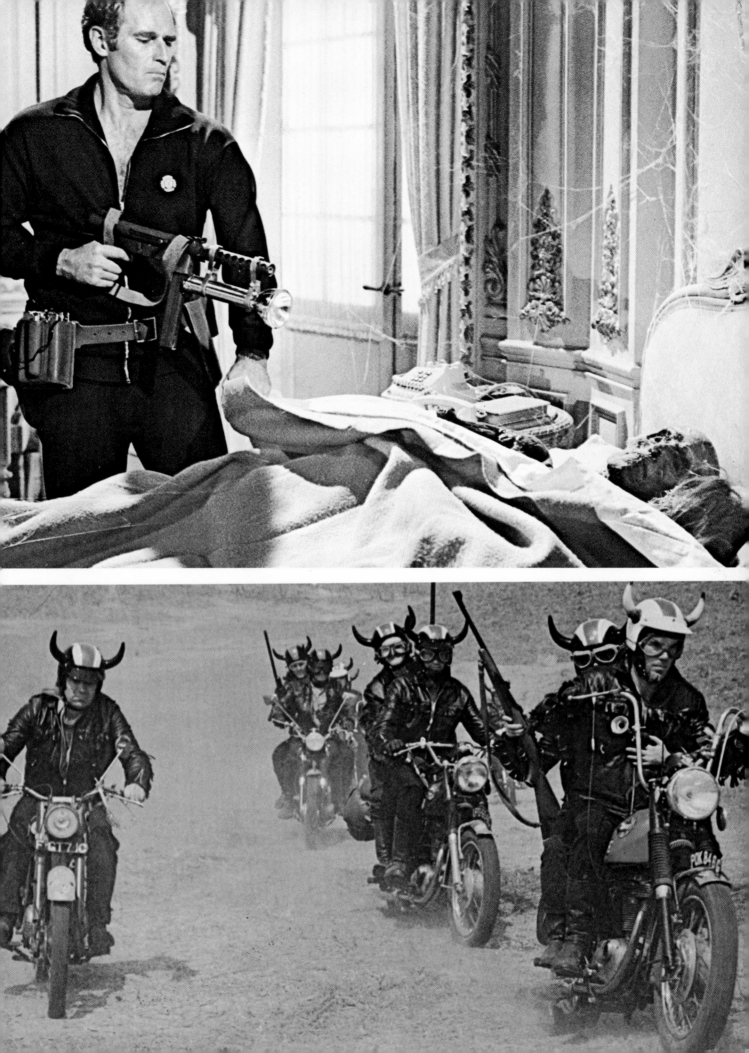

destruct mechanism is too efficient to be switched off.

In all other respects, of course, the films are exact opposites. Kubrick's *Dr Strangelove* (1963), with its parenthetical title *or: How I Learned to Stop Worrying and Love the Bomb*, was dominated by Peter Sellers in three guises, by Terry Southern's brutal comic writing, and by the gigantic sets designed by Ken Adam. Taking its cue from the rise of television satire, the film sought to defuse the Bomb by ridicule, finally packing it on its way with Slim Pickens joyfully aboard and Vera Lynn on the soundtrack. If nobody's going to do anything about Doomsday, it suggested, we might as well greet it in good humour – and so we do, with real tears in our eyes. Packed with good things, like the performances of Keenan Wynn and Sterling Hayden and the extraordinary vision of Dr Strangelove himself battling with the prosthetic hand that aches to snap into a Nazi salute, the film gave the sensation at the time that we were enjoying our last cigarette before facing the firing squad.

With Sidney Lumet's *Fail Safe* (1964), there was no room for laughter, although the equivalent to Strangelove was present in the form of Walter Matthau coolly advising that the unexpected advantage in the nuclear balance should be exploited unhesitatingly: 'These are Marxist fanatics, not normal people. Do nothing, and

(opposite, above and below) Dana Andrews faces the effects of the *Crack in the World* (Paramount, 1965). (above) Slim Pickens clears the bomb-bay in *Dr Strangelove* (Columbia, 1963). (below) The magnificent set for the War Room in the same film.

they'll surrender. We'll never have a chance like this again.' On the hot line was Henry Fonda, filmed Lumet-style in searching close-up against a neutral background and bearing the scrutiny with his usual anguished calm. The film tipped occasionally into melodrama, for all its low-key production, with Dan O'Herlihy continuing his nightmares from *Invasion USA*, involving a bullfight and a high-pitched whine, and administering the *coup de grâce* to New York in terrible compensation for the destruction of Moscow. The final title stated that the US Defence Department confirmed the system couldn't fail in this manner, but it was not a point on which the audience could feel reassured.

Then there was *The War Game* (1965) which Peter Watkins made for the BBC but which they preferred to release theatrically rather than risk panic from the uninformed viewer. It was a mistaken decision, not only because the film's faults were magnified by the large screen but also because a programme considered too disturbing for British television could scarcely be permitted to appear among the programmes of some implicitly tougher nation. To date, not one sequence of the film has been televised anywhere in the world,

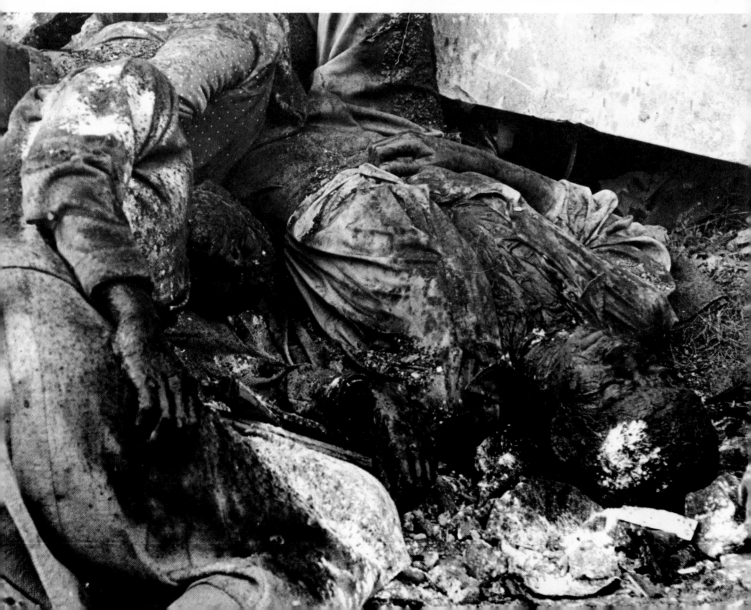

Victims of the deluge. (left) Piggy (Hugh Edwards) and Ralph (James Aubrey) in Peter Brook's *Lord of the Flies* (Allen-Hodgdon Productions and Two Arts, 1963). (below) A pile of corpses from Peter Watkins' *The War Game* (BBC TV, 1965), with remarkable makeup by Lilias Munro.

himself) knows about the dying children, the buckets of collected wedding rings, the execution squads, he has no intention of sharing their fate. Instead, the destruction of Los Angeles finds him heading for his country hide-out in the family trailer, seizing weapons along the way and using them unhesitatingly to discourage any opposition; his family is horrified at the change in his personality, but an attack by young thugs and the rape of his daughter quickly persuades them that the gunplay is justified. By contrast with *War Game*, which shows a complete social collapse into lassitude and inaction, *Panic* shows at the end that Milland's ruthlessness has paid off – he has maintained the family unit long enough to be able to reach the safety of an official rehabilitation group.

In the sense that it regards nuclear war as a temporary inconvenience, the sort of unpleasantness that will blow over if you stay cool and keep your hat on, *Panic* is undoubtedly an accurate picture of average illusions, showing all the faith in Higher Authority that *War Game* scorns. However sceptical we may be about such confidence, it is strangely rare in disaster films, which prefer to celebrate, with some glee, the total eradication of the past, plus the repudiation of the immediate present. What matters is the future, usually heralded by the end title proclaiming 'The Beginning'. It may look a little complicated out there, runs the message, but it can't be worse than the world that's just been blown away.

There is nothing reactionary about Roger Corman's first science-fiction film, *The Day the World Ended* (1955), in which seven survivors are whittled down to two by radiation, argument and a beaky mutant that is killed at last by a purifying downpour. 'Rick, you've given me a sense of responsibility towards the future of our kind,' says the girl, as they leave the steaming remains behind and set off presumably to propagate like mad. Less conveniently, *The World, the Flesh and the Devil* (1958) concludes with Inger Stevens, Mel Ferrer and Harry Belafonte setting off for a new life together after fighting their way picturesquely through the deserted streets of New York. Unlike Baldwin Sr, they realize (largely thanks to the United Nations) that shooting each other will merely perpetuate an outmoded tradition. A threesome does, admittedly, offer more rewarding possibilities – and at least one of them can sing.

In Europe, survival films seem on the whole to have been less sprightly, possibly because the Continent offers less room actually to survive in. Peter Brook's *Lord of the Flies* (1963), closely following William Golding's novel about the savagery and ritual of a group of schoolboys cast away on a desert island (after, it's hinted, the breakout of war), pictures the erosion of conventional behaviour with a fine sense of nightmare. The story has links with Moreau as the children degenerate into animal-like savagery, inventing new

which effectively muffled any chance it had of influencing political opinion; nevertheless, it won an Oscar, and found wide distribution in the West. On a personal level, its horrific portrait of the effects of a nuclear bomb on a town in Kent was enough to confirm to many thousands of people that such a war must never happen. On a political level, the only clear result seems to have been a change in the British Government's budget allocation for Civil Defence. It was slashingly reduced.

As science fiction, *The War Game* simulated a documentary approach to show the near future, using anonymous non-actors being interviewed for their opinions even in the middle of a fire-storm. Statistics and quotations illustrating the inadequacies and ill-preparedness of the country for any such crisis are sprinkled through the film, merging supposition with fact, combining conjecture with prophecy. As with all Watkins's work, the film bristles with outrage and in its clumsy attempts to score points it sometimes falls flat on its face, but the faults act as a unique support to authenticity and lend it an undeniable power. It lacks charm, style, restraint, rhythm and balance, and manages perfectly well without any of them. What it flings at its audience is conviction, to be ignored at their peril.

The same could not be said of *Panic in Year Zero* (1962), the closest American equivalent to *The War Game*, but it was in some ways an easier film to tolerate. Directed with bland efficiency by Ray Milland and based on two Ward Moore stories (*Lot* and *Lot's Daughter*), it wasted no time complaining about the Bomb and its victims; if Baldwin Sr (played by Milland

(left) Dandy Nicholls as Mrs Ethel Shroake, the only traceable heir to the British throne, in *The Bed Sitting Room* (United Artists, 1969).
(right) Howard Keel, Janina Fay and Nicole Maurey confront a homicidal plant in *The Day of the Triffids* (Allied Artists, 1963).

codes of existence as their public-school upbringing merges with the demands of their new environment. They don't charge around with guns, but spears are just as effective, and the message is the same: the Bomb may offer a Beginning, but if so we'll be starting at the Beginning, having inherited not culture but pure animal instinct.

By contrast, the rituals of the past preserve a firm grip on the actions of the pathetic community in *The Bed Sitting Room* (1969), Richard Lester's compassionate if erratic version of the Milligan/Antrobus play. World War III, over in two-and-a-half minutes, has left scars of mental discontinuity on the British survivors, slowly starving in a landscape of ashes and filth. They attempt gallantly to keep up appearances, clinging to the conventional phrases ('Mustn't grumble') for a few shreds of comfort, and watching television with close attention whenever the man with the BBC voice, the top half of a dinner jacket, and an empty television frame, offers a news bulletin. Radiation being what it is, Ralph Richardson turns into a bed-sitting room, Mona Washbourne into a wardrobe and Arthur Lowe into a parrot, while Rita Tushingham gives birth to a short-lived monstrosity but prepares with fortitude for the next attempt. Ruthlessly lumbered with an interminable music track, the film shows signs of having tried to please too many production interests, but its livid settings and wrecked characters, dimly saluting their new Queen (Mrs Ethel Shroake), are as horrifying as those of *The War Game*.

As might be expected from the director of *La Grande Bouffe*, Marco Ferreri's picture of the end of the world is both bizarre and brutal; he made *The Seed of Man* (1969) for Italian television, who evidently demanded a few restraints but were taken aback by the rape, cannibalism and absent-minded violence of the finished product. Starring Anne Wiazemsky and Annie Girardot, the film is set on a sea-shore where the decaying mound of a beached whale provides shade and a temporary source of food (as well as a symbol for the death of civilization). It's one of those stories in which the potent male has suddenly become a rarity, and the Amazonian Miss Girardot is consequently on the man-hunt; filmed in bleached, chilly colours, her search appears depressingly pointless. Equally depressing was Jan Schmidt's *The End of August at the Ozone Hotel* (1965), in which another band of women gallops about the countryside in search of men, finding only one old-timer, well past his prime. Shot in dark monochrome, the film makes the most of its incongruities – the new generation staring uncomprehendingly at the useless furnishings of the old – but never quite lives up to its romantic title.

Although the works of John Wyndham and John Christopher are the popular classics of the disaster story (with Christopher's *Cloud on Silver*, in particular, showing clear links with *Lord of the Flies*), neither writer has been too well served by the cinema on this theme (Wyndham's alien children have had better luck). The film of *The Day of the Triffids* (1963) blew all its chances on poor special effects and rambling vegetables, dissipating the hallucinatory claustrophobia of Wyndham's extremely visual original descriptions of a world turned blind and plagued with lethal plants.

Rather more interesting was Cornel Wilde's *No Blade of Grass* (1970), in which Nigel Davenport and Jean Wallace struggle across a polluted countryside, attacked occasionally by motor-cycling marauders in Viking helmets, and murder their way into a stronghold of conservation. Primitive and well-meaning, the film delivers the customary accusations of atheism and neglect, heavily disguised as entertainment.

Better, it would seem, to forget about the accusations and stick to the entertainment. The wishful-thinking aspects of being the only man alive in a world full of women provide an entertaining diversion from the usual post-atomic gloom, and science fiction has tinkered with the idea several times (notably in Pat Frank's *Mr Adam* and Philip Wylie's fascinating *The Disappearance*). In the cinema, the orgiastic implications have been ignored; when Fox made *The Last Man on Earth* in a silent tinted version in 1924, based on John D. Swain's story of a disease that kills all men over 14 except one, it resolved itself into a humorous study of the effect this would have on politics. In 1933, the whole thing was filmed again with music, and called *It's Great to Be Alive* – one hopes with good reason.

Sidney Salkow's *The Last Man on Earth* (1964), however, was of a different breed. The film was an American-Italian co-production based on Richard Matheson's harrowing novel *I Am Legend*, and it featured Vincent Price as the sole survivor of a plague that has turned his neighbours into vampires. At night he sits in his barricaded house with the record-player turned up as they roam around outside; by day, he ventures out with hammer and sharpened stakes to kill as many of them as possible before nightfall. It's a magnificent idea, repeating once more the Matheson theme of the beleaguered individual, and the film makes a modest attempt to live up to it with the opening sequences of the vampire-hunter patrolling the cluttered streets; later, haste has evidently set in, and the whole production gets ugly and banal, despite Vincent Price's attempts to maintain the balance.

In 1971, the story returned in the guise of *The Omega Man*, directed by Boris Sagal, in which the vampire concept has sadly vanished, and the plague-carriers (victims of a Sino-Russian germ war) are simply unable to tolerate strong light, or, it seems, Charlton Heston's flamboyant apartment. The sharpened stakes and the garlic are replaced by a matter-of-fact machine-gun, and Heston's opponents are little more than albino psychotics in modish dark glasses, sprinting impishly about like Chaucerian friars. Forgivable as it may be to simplify the technology-versus-humanity debate in this fashion, the film reveals its true colours depressingly quickly with Heston's screening of his favourite movie – *Woodstock*, no less – in which the garbled hopes of peace-lovers are evidently intended to encapsulate both the innocence and the naivety of the common man. Yet somehow *The Omega Man* retains something of

Matheson's compulsiveness: the customary garbage of disaster is as fascinating as ever – the empty city, the untended houses, the corpse-filled hospital beds, the eerie menace of torch-bearers in the streets at night. Sometimes, if nowhere near often enough, the film has an authentic chill to offer. But perhaps one day there'll be a wholly successful version of what Matheson wrote in the first place.

With Roger Corman, not surprisingly, the controversial survivor was *The Last Woman on Earth* (1960), a rattlingly commercial title attached to a complex, introverted story about Harold, Evelyn and Martin in Puerto Rico. While they're skin-diving, a poisonous gas kills everyone above water, leaving them plenty of room to fight in earnest over who's to look after Evelyn. There is a superb high-angle shot as they wander down a sun-baked street littered with corpses, but the spectacular aspects of the situation are on the whole ignored; as can be detected from the final confrontation in a church, Corman had other things on his mind (it was one of those years when he made six films). Yet the end of the world was never far

(previous pages) Elaine Giftos (left) and Robert Corff (right), the new senior citizens in a society depleted by a nerve gas fatal to everybody over the age of 25. A scene from Roger Corman's *Gas-s-s! or it became necessary to destroy the world in order to save it.* (AIP, 1970).

(left) Vincent Price in search of vampires in *The Last Man on Earth* (Associated Productions/ Produzione La Regina, 1964).

from his thoughts; in 1958, he had made the fondly remembered *Teenage Caveman*, in which Robert Vaughn and a tiny cast working valiantly to appear a large one discovered that their Stone Age existence had been brought about by the Bomb; this in turn explains the mutant nature of the prehistoric monsters they've hitherto encountered. 'How many times will it happen again?' asks the commentary as they gape incredulously. 'Will there be survivors next time, or will it be the end?'

The best of the next times turned out to be *Gas-s-s! or it became necessary to destroy the world in order to save it* (1970), in which the planet is polluted with a poison that kills everybody over 25 of instant old age. As the US President says on television shortly before he dies, it's a human error anybody could have made. Played as black comedy, the film turns society completely on its head, with the Hell's Angels protecting the old way of life while the football-playing all-American boys drive around in dune buggies attacking girls and ransacking houses. Country Joe and the Fish provide the music, and there are occasional comments from

God and Edgar Allan Poe who storms about the countryside on a Harley-Davidson, with the Raven on his shoulder and Lenore riding pillion. The script had been written for United Artists, but they decided it couldn't be filmed for less than two million dollars; so Corman, true to form, bought it back and made it himself in four weeks for less than 300,000 dollars. It was, he said, a film he firmly believed in; and although it has an indulgent free-wheeling style at odds with his usually more controlled technique, one can see why it mattered to him.

Armageddon has passed, leaving the planet to the young, just as they always knew it would; after taking due stock of the alternative societies that might be derived from the ruins of America, they create their own. It is populated with heroes – Kennedy, Nehru, Guevara, Alfred E. Neuman – and despite its resemblance to a hippie commune shows signs of lasting stability. Lavish with music, colour and euphoria, *Gas-s-s!* seizes cheerfully on the end of the world and draws the refreshing conclusion that it has already happened. From now on, things can only get better.

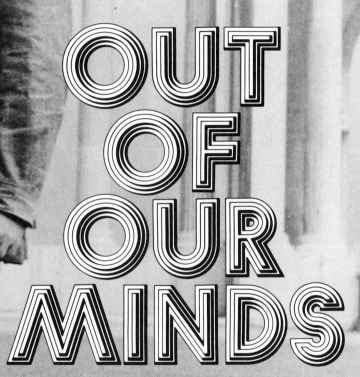

OUT OF OUR MINDS

Ask yourself, What do we want in this country above all? People want to be happy, isn't that right? Haven't you heard it all your life? I want to be happy, people say. Well, aren't they? Don't we keep them moving, don't we give them fun? That's all we live for, isn't it? For pleasure, for titillation? And you must admit our culture provides plenty of these. The Fire Chief.

Contrary to the supposition of those who never read it, the function of science fiction is not that of a crystal ball. Its writers are not astrologers, divining the events of the next decade by extrapolating from those of the last, consulting horoscopes and casting runes. They are under no obligation to forecast correctly, or to forecast at all, and they keep no score-cards on which to balance their correct and incorrect predictions like students of some fourth-dimensional roulette wheel. In fact, they can seldom be drawn to make *any* specific claims about the years ahead, even though, like Heinlein with his 'Future History', they may for convenience draw up a rough chart of probable events from which other, decreasingly probable events might be derived. Such a chart helps to keep a series of related

headlong upon us with new and unimagined headlines, or feared and long-avoided events, accidents, oblivions. So science fiction seeks to anticipate the unknown, to shape a utopian future from a changed and improved present (discovering in the process that improvements are not necessarily for the better, nor utopianism the ideal form of existence). And if perfection is constantly elusive, since few people can agree on what's perfect and what isn't, science fiction most frequently points the way by describing a society that cries out for change – a society not dissimilar from any you care to think of that exists in the world today.

Struggling to find its feet during the first twenty years of its existence, the cinema was not an ideal format for political debate until the use of film as propaganda

(previous pages) Winston Smith at the crossroads: Edmond O'Brien in Michael Anderson's *1984* (ABPC, 1956).

(left) Edmond O'Brien and Jan Sterling consider the alternatives in *1984*.
(right) The fight to stay human; Kevin McCarthy and Dana Wynter flee from the *Invasion of the Body Snatchers* (Allied Artists, 1955).

stories approximately consistent with each other, but that it should be consistent with reality when the present catches up with the writer's future is a bonus as fortuitous as it is unexpected. The whole point of a novel like *Dr Strangelove* or *1984* is that the events it describes should *not* happen.

Like the cinema, science fiction reflects what is uppermost in the popular mind. Its mood is drawn from the headlines of the immediate past, the images that have sleeted across the writer's vision and been juggled into a confetti of fantasies and conjectures before being cast out in the form of words on paper. And because the experiences of the past are controllable, available for shuffling and reshuffling like a pack of cards, the future, by contrast, is an area of the *un*controllable, rushing

became effective in the hands of D. W. Griffith. Previously, glimpses of the future were strictly on the level of gadgets, rocket flights, or Dante's Inferno. But Griffith learned how to manipulate images to create an urgent mosaic of concern about moral problems, as he did with *Intolerance* (1916), and after this the cinema could tackle anything. For the first major onslaught in science fiction terms, however, we must look again to *Metropolis* (1926), where Orwell's proles are brought to life in Lang's trudging battalions of identical workers, twenty years before *1984* was published. These dead-eyed, robotic figures, mercilessly exploited by the trivial idlers of Metropolis, made an extraordinarily potent image; gullible, expendable, industrious, they did exactly what they were told – a rare and stabilizing virtue for as long as it lasts.

Once World War II had made it apparent that obeying orders without question could have personal as well as national disadvantages, the *Metropolis* example slowly began to be taken up in parallel with the alien invasion and atomic warning films of the '50s. With the growing suspicion that those entrusted with government were not necessarily best suited to handle it, with McCarthy hunting witches and Presley blasting out a generation gap, blank-faced figures, their minds directed by malignant and subversive powers, infiltrated the cinemas of the West. When Orwell's 1949 novel became a best-seller, it was a foregone conclusion that *1984* would be filmed, and it duly appeared in 1955, bowdlerized, anaesthetized, and with a happy ending

Snatchers, which Don Siegel turned into his best-ever film in 1955.

Although, at the time, *Invasion of the Body Snatchers* looked like a host of other science-fiction movies – the small-town setting, the undistinguished cast, the 'possession' theme (from such as *Invaders from Mars* or *It Came from Outer Space*) – it stands out in retrospect for its many brilliantly horrific moments, as when Kevin McCarthy discovers his own nearly completed double growing in the greenhouse, and transfixes it with a garden fork. Aliens are taking over by growing imitation people in pods, and absorbing the minds and memories of the originals while they sleep; they offer an untroubled world: 'No love, no emotion, desire, ambition, or faith – without them, life is so simple'.

in which love and revolt still smoulder beneath the blowing leaves. Edmond O'Brien was Winston Smith, a role of stocky non-conformism that has adhered to his screen presence ever since, while Michael Redgrave was more convincing – and more Orwellian – as his chilly inquisitor. Like John Halas's animated version of *Animal Farm* (1954), which made Orwell's parable into a troubling cartoon, *1984* did not spearhead the uneasiness of the time, it merely echoed it – just as Van Vogt, Bradbury, and other writers had been tackling the theme of totalitarianism in concert with Orwell in the 1940s. It was the time of Heinlein's *Puppet Masters* (filmed inauspiciously as *The Brain Eaters* in 1958), of Bradbury's *Fahrenheit 451* (which had to wait until 1966), and of Jack Finney's *Invasion of the Body*

But McCarthy isn't interested in the simple life: 'In my practice I've seen how people have allowed their humanity to drain away . . . all of us, we harden our hearts, grow callous. Only when we have to fight to stay human do we realize how precious it is.' At the end, when his own girl has been converted to an unfeeling automaton, he screams impotently on a highway crowded with impersonal vehicles, spreading pods across the country. 'I felt surrounded by pods,' Siegel says of his Hollywood life in the 1950s, 'and sometimes I still do.'

Other pods followed (among them, for example, the victims of *The Brain from Planet Arous* in 1958, headed by John Agar who went through a great deal in this era), but the next great breakthrough came unexpectedly from John Frankenheimer and George Axelrod, the creators of *The Manchurian Candidate* (1962). Intelligent, funny, superbly written, beautifully played and brilliantly directed, it was a study of the all-embracing fantasy in everyday social, emotional and political existence. A Chinese plot to take over America with the help of brainwashed GIs begins to fall apart when Frank Sinatra, recovering his memory in fragments, notices that Laurence Harvey, son of Angela Lansbury, is nowhere near as lovable as everybody thinks. The classic sequence is the indoctrination nightmare which keeps turning into a Ladies' Gardening Club; other treasures include the karate battle with Henry Silva, the Convention at which James Gregory nearly

was open to the suggestion that his marriage was a farce. It took his presence as midwife while Mary Ure gave birth on a houseboat to bring him to his senses again. Like so many Bogarde vehicles, this one gave the impression that it would have been intolerable without him, but the shots of the dark underwater figure, cut off from all sensation, had a suitably macabre quality. In Italy, the aliens returned in Camillo Bazzoni's remarkable trilogy of short films, *L'Invasione* (1964), *L'Urlo* (1965) and *La Caduta di Varema* (1966), photographed in a torrent of tracking shots, pans and zooms by Bertolucci's cameraman Vittorio Storaro. The restless undercurrent of the films is a paranoid certainty that dehumanization, rapid and unnoticed, has actually

(right) Cyril Cusack and Oskar Werner aboard the fire-engine in Francois Truffaut's *Fahrenheit 451* (Universal, 1966).

becomes President, and a scene with Leslie Parrish in fancy dress. To Frankenheimer's delight the film incensed both the American Legion *and* the Communist party ('After all, the whole point of the film was the absurdity of any type of extremism, left or right'). But it was the scene of the assassination that gave the film its lasting importance, appearing, as events unfolded, to be an uncanny forecast of the death of a President. As if continuing to bear out the truth of the film, the White House after 1963 became increasingly associated with the irrational, the repressive, and the deceitful.

In Britain, the brainwashing was a modest affair: Dirk Bogarde got plunged into a tank of water in Basil Dearden's *The Mind Benders* (1963) and after eight hours

overtaken mankind. For *L'Invasione*, the aliens (who can be recognized by their huge sunglasses) appear with grim dedication in the classroom, the police force and the Church, preaching that honesty, morality and conscience do not exist. But by *L'Urlo* the blame has been placed squarely with humanity itself; Bazzoni looks ahead – not too far – to a state in which the population, drugged from infancy, is completely without either emotion, sentiment or 'harmful individuality' of any kind.

The Winston Smith in this context is a citizen who has managed to evade the injections that maintain zombiehood and commits such crimes as reading poetry, listening to classical music, helping a sick man in the street and falling in love with a girl. 'Take him away,' she says, promptly, to the television camera that spies on their meeting, and he is hunted down by the state police and sentenced to mental conditioning. In the third film, *The Fall of Varema*, the petrification of society has reached its final stages; Bazzoni gives us fragmentary illustrations – abandoned buildings, deserted streets, and at nightfall the frequent outbursts of gunfire as citizens hunt each other down in bitter hatred. Once again the only comfort is the hint that love might find a way to survive, but it seems a small chance.

The moment of realization that apparently normal people are doing totally abnormal things is the shock

that never fails in science fiction. In *It Came from Outer Space*, it's the moment when a man looks directly into the sun without blinking; in *Invasion of the Body Snatchers*, it's the placid scene of townsfolk unloading pods in the main square. In his earliest venture into science fiction, the French director Jean-Luc Godard made splendid use of this 'double-take' technique; it was a twenty-minute episode called *Le Nouveau Monde* (1962), made for inclusion in the Italian film *Rogopag*, and it consisted of a young man in Paris becoming gradually aware that everything has changed during his recent absence. Passers-by obsessively swallow pills, conversations follow no logical pattern, the names of everyday objects appear to have changed;

more tellingly, the Eiffel Tower has lost its top half, the Arc de Triomphe has lost its arch, and the girls in the swimming-pool carry knives for protection. It seems that these are some of the consequences of a local atomic explosion which (in keeping with physicist Werner Heisenberg's astonishing theory of atomic structure) has eradicated cause and effect.

The city in which normal rules of logic and feeling no longer apply is of course Paris, and Godard expanded his simple but potent metaphor to create the ultra-modern Alphaville, Capital of Pain, in 1965. The film was made in the hotels, offices and streets of Paris, without sets, gadgets or the traditional impediments of science fiction – but it looked unearthly, it looked solid, and it looked amazingly real. Superficially, *Alphaville* is a private-eye yarn, in which the granite-faced Lemmy Caution is sent to locate a missing agent and to eradicate a dangerous scientist in a city-state ruled by the computer Alpha 60. After hurling a number of opponents through the furniture and outwitting the computer by behaving illogically, Caution completes his mission and leaves the place in chaos, taking with him Natasha von Braun (as usual with Godard, the name is selected with care), a girl he has rescued from Alpha 60's control. Godard's purpose with this plot is to comment on the stranglehold maintained by both political and scientific machinery on the social mind, causing conformism and atrophy. Yet the film is also his most Hitchcockian work, in its use of violence, its use of the journey as a structural and symbolic pivot, and in its concern with the rescue of a girl against her will from the forces which are imprisoning her. Above all, it is a study of words and meanings; as in *L'Invasione* such terms as 'conscience' and 'tenderness' are being outlawed, since they have no sense in a computer's programming, and if they cannot be expressed there's a good chance that they will cease to exist as human qualities.

In Godard's subsequent science-fiction films, the importance of language continues to be argued. His 1967 episode for *The Oldest Profession* (another subject repeatedly examined in his work) was called *The Year 2000*, by which date, according to Godard, Sentimental and Physical Love would be entirely separate areas of specialization among prostitutes. It takes a visitor from another galaxy to point out that the mouth is designed both for speech and for love. Although played by Jacques Charrier, the alien is clearly the spokesman for Godard himself, angrily watching the world go to hell in its own way and aware of the persistent futility of using mere words to try and stop it (increasingly, from 1967, his films were to feature extremes of bloodshed as a desperate visual argument). In the same year, he made *Weekend*, in which large chunks of dialogue are obscured completely – by monotonous music, by heavily amplified traffic noises, or by the Wellesian trick of getting everybody to talk at once.

With this brutal piling of noise upon noise, Godard forces his audience to realize a double tragedy – first, that his characters can't get through to one another, and second, that if they could their speech would still be worthless. Mireille Darc sits on a table in her underwear telling a long story about what seems to have been an orgy including the unorthodox use of eggs (later an egg is put to explicitly unconventional use in a bizarre sacrificial rite involving a passing nude), and her voice is increasingly drowned by random noises. Later, as the film goes on a nightmare outing through weekend roads littered with crushed vehicles, glass, blood and sprawled bodies, Godard's horror at the imbecility of the human memory – recalling an orgy in immense detail while shrugging off everyday corpses as no more than a driving hazard – becomes our own. *Weekend* is a work of grim fury, itself almost inarticulate with the frustrations of existing in a world that makes no sense. If science fiction may be regarded as the necessary language for dealing with the unspeakable, this is one of the great films in science-fiction cinema.

Godard's contemporary, François Truffaut, was less successful with *his* exploration of a brain-washed society, but the awkwardnesses of *Fahrenheit 451* (1966) have too often been allowed to overshadow its merits (again linked with Hitchcock, and particularly with *Vertigo*). If one can forget Ray Bradbury's original and see the film as the expression of Truffaut's viewpoint, it immediately makes sense as a study of loneliness. Like his delinquent (in *400 Blows*), his musician (in *Shoot the Pianist*), his elusive heroine (in *Jules and Jim* and many more) and his married man (in *Silken Skin*), Truffaut's fireman is on the hunt for a real self, a hunt of which he only gradually becomes aware through his encounters with others making similar journeys. On the one hand is his wife Linda, immersing herself in the television 'family' which even addresses her by name. On the other is Clarisse, the appealing girl from next door who parallels his wife's narcissism by wondering why society won't accept her. Both roles are taken by Julie Christie, a piece of casting which at one stroke reveals and emphasizes one of the most important patterns of the Bradbury original.

Sadly, the balance is missed by the film's deletion of Faber, the old man who is Montag's ally in the second half of the book, and who is Bradbury's 'outsider' equivalent to the Fire Chief. The paternalistic aspects of the Chief, an omniscient bantam who consigns 'Mein Kampf' to the flames with honeyed reassurances but is also nervously dependent upon the loyalty of his staff, are well brought out by the film – and they're in keeping with one of Bradbury's most persistent themes, the adored but elusive father. Truffaut uses a tiny scene near the end of the film to acknowledge this, with an old man dying as his son haltingly recites the words his father taught him. The same paternalism,

one might argue, is implicit in Montag's response to literature; he is simply exchanging one authority for another when he takes to reading books instead of burning them, which is no doubt why Truffaut gives him the air of a monkish pedant rather than that of an enthusiastic convert.

If there is an ultimate irony in that Montag 'becomes' someone else, at least he is better off, Truffaut suggests, than are his previous co-zombies who have no identity at all save that stamped upon them by the ultra-Platonic city-state. It's a chilly message, particularly in its snowbound final scenes where the muted landscape colours are appropriately more easy on the eye than the nursery-bright hues of the earlier sequences; as the bookmen (who save literary classics by committing them to memory) tramp along the lakeside, muttering to themselves like madmen, they may well have all the diversity of books in a very public library but there seems little chance of their ever being 'read'. Bradbury's ending blew the city sky-high on the horizon, but Truffaut leaves the stainless mausoleum intact, and with it remains the inference that the bookmen may never cease to be socially redundant. At least their self-sacrifice is a matter of personal choice, whereas their city cousins never had access to alternatives. It's some consolation, as is much of the film's technique, with Bernard Herrmann's music (another Hitchcock allegiance) accompanying the delightful shots of the fire-engine scooting through the countryside like a child's dream come true, or the book-burning scenes in which the flames pore fascinatedly over the pages in hypnotic close-up. Truffaut has wisely let the books speak for themselves, and they are marvellously eloquent.

In *Fahrenheit 451*, society has lost its edge from an excess of good intentions; no malice is implied, simply the over-zealous pursuit of happiness. The actions of governments are seldom interpreted in such philanthropic terms on the screen, which customarily insists that bureaucracy is built upon a mound of mistakes and cover-ups, violently administered. The symbolic aliens of the 1950s were replaced by the savage authoritarians of the 1960s, trampling on freedom, high spirits and young love in such films as *Zabriskie Point* or *Bonnie and Clyde*. The new generation of pods, taking its cue from the newspapers, was also more violent, the most disturbing example being George A. Romero's *Night of the Living Dead* (1968), in which the victims of Government carelessness (a space probe has tainted the atmosphere) are not surprisingly out for the blood of those not yet affected. The film centres on a

Population control: (above) The riot police shovel away a rebellion in *Soylent Green* (MGM, 1973). (right) James Caan becomes an unexpected hero by surviving the game of *Rollerball* (United Artists, 1975).

small group of 'normals' barricaded in a country house while zombies roam outside, refusing to die from the jagged wounds of shotgun blasts. The siege is a traditional one, but it breaks the rules: the invaders turn up inside the house as well, and there is some appalling cannibalism in the cellar, all flashing implements, piercing shrieks and splashing gore. When the US Cavalry arrives in the form of a local posse, it is unable to distinguish between zombies and 'normals', so *everybody* gets demolished. The savagery of *Night of the Living Dead*, presented through amateurish performances and rough-hewn photography and editing, is cumulatively intolerable – but like *The War Game* it makes its point from sheer ferocity. The world has gone beyond reason and decency, and somebody's going to have to pay. Probably us.

After a couple of less successful 'straight' films, Romero returned to the subject with *The Crazies* (1973), which though technically a well-made production was received with only moderate enthusiasm by the critics, jaded by the imitations that had closely followed *Living Dead*. One example of the latter was *I Drink Your Blood* (1971), in which a hippie gang is infected with rabies and goes gorily berserk; it took a lot of beating. Another was *Rage* (1972), starring and directed by George C. Scott, gradually dying from a nerve-gas accident while the authorities attempt a massive cover-up. In *The Crazies*, it's a germ-warfare virus that gets scattered across a small town, turning the inhabitants insane before killing them; the symptoms of insanity are less noticeable than the presence of the Army, which cordons off the area and starts mopping up before anybody has a clue what's going on. Not surprisingly, insane or not, the citizens fight back. Romero has a tremendous time with this gruesome chaos, showing people placidly mowing the lawn or playing the piano as their neighbours are shot to pieces around them. In one scene, soldiers fight their way into a house to find a dear old lady sitting upstairs doing her knitting. Smiling in welcome at her first rescuer, she transfixes him with a knitting-needle.

A whole subdivision of science fiction deals with this kind of domestic hostility. It was formalized by Robert Sheckley in his story *Seventh Victim* which, with the accumulation of a corpse or two, turned up as Elio Petri's *Tenth Victim* in 1965. In a completely dehumanized future, the Big Hunt Ministry (a safety valve for latent aggressive instincts) sets citizens against each other in legal duels to the death; each highly trained participant alternates as 'hunter' and 'victim', aiming for the ten-kill score that will bring unlimited political and financial privileges. Ursula Andress is a top contender with her lethal rapid-fire brassière, while Marcello Mastroianni favours exploding spurs; Elsa Martinelli, in some tantalizing costumes, is somewhat neglected on the sidelines. Salvo Randone makes the most impact, growling briefly behind an

armoury of prosthetics as the owner of a killer-training gymnasium. The film is never quite as much fun as it should be, but Di Venanzo's photography gives it a rich glow of pop-art colour, and there are pleasing touches such as a library whose classics include a first-edition *Flash Gordon* and an 'antique' pin-table that is part of one room's décor. By the 1970s, predictably, these signposts to the 21st century were already well-worn landmarks.

Jules Feiffer's play *Little Murders*, first performed in 1967, also appeared almost conventional by the time it reached the screen in 1971. Directed by Alan Arkin

The release of aggressive instincts: (above) Ursula Andress protects Marcello Mastroianni in *Tenth Victim* (Champion Films and Les Films Concordia, 1965).
(opposite above) The sacrificial image of Paul Jones (above) dominates a fascist rally in *Privilege* (Universal, 1967). (opposite below) Adrienne Corri is raped by Alex and his Droogs in Kubrick's *A Clockwork Orange* (Warners, 1971).

and starring Elliott Gould, it featured a typical American family, sheltering from the snipers outside behind steel shutters and appalled that their lovely daughter should be married without God being mentioned at the ceremony. As an hysterical picture of what would happen if the forces of law and order *didn't* act brutally, it expressed Feiffer's customary schizophrenia, and acted as a counterweight to George Lucas's *THX 1138* (1969), in which the Thought Police were once again on patrol. Their delinquent opponent this time is the shaven-headed Robert Duvall, known as THX 1138 or Thex for short, who has been driven to rebellion by the loss of his mate, Luh. They had recently discovered sex, which is forbidden and practically unknown thanks to everyone's daily drug intake, and Luh has been liquidated after becoming pregnant.

As an extra spur, to rouse Thex from conformity, his cell-mate had deliberately given him the wrong drug ration. What put the idea in her head is not clear, but it could be something to do with Donald Pleasence (it usually is), who claims to have found a way to manipulate the gigantic central computer to suit his own purposes, and seems to have plans for Thex as potential revolutionary material. Or it could be just a general conviction that human nature will survive any conditioning process somehow and that vague flickers of love have illuminated Luh's purpose. Science fiction is forever pointing out the risks within an environment controlling technology, and the fringes of Thex's world are haunted by stunted predators who scavenge from the society that excludes them, while unstable equipment and inefficient operators cause frequent explosions in the workshops. In one sudden sequence (anticipating the lethal breakdowns of *Westworld*), a robot walks joltingly into a wall, backs off, tries again, and keeps trying until someone notices the malfunction. Another shot, naggingly brief, shows a lizard patrolling some electric cables; it illustrates the impossibility of exterminating *all* random factors. And what finally allows Thex his getaway is the computation that the task-force allocated to pursue him has exceeded its budget and must accordingly be recalled.

Coming out of Francis Ford Coppola's Zoetrope studio, *THX 1138* is often stunning to look at, not because it glitters with hardware but because it so frequently disposes of sets completely and encases its characters in plain white. Cast into prison, Thex becomes one of a tiny handful of criminals adrift in a bleached vacuum where the only colour is the flesh of face and hands; distances are incalculable and darkness is unknown. With its futile scufflings and impotent speeches endlessly repeated, the scene is reminiscent of Samuel Beckett. Like all the best science fiction, too, the film has a sense of humour; the mechanical cops are its happiest invention, their heads glowing chromium, their voices mellow with reassurance. Seemingly unaware of any hostile intentions on the part of their quarry, they offer help and rescue at all times, even when breaking down doors or applying pole-like weapons that paralyse the senses. In the background, a blandly cheerful commentary assesses tolerance levels of men being 'conditioned', genially gives the statistics of the latest disaster, and answers a steady stream of calls for advice with the phrase 'What's wrong?', spoken as though nothing ever took more than a few seconds to put right. When Thex goes to his daily confessional to dispose of any worries he may have, he is interrupted by words of encouragement and sympathy in a meaningless flow.

Curiously enough, Thex's victory, clawing his way up through the underground levels until he staggers into the open air, seems somewhat unrewarding – even ungrateful in the face of all this well-meaning effort to please. A huge oval sunset behind him, sinking like a punctured balloon, silhouettes his indecision as the credits roll and the occasional bird wallows overhead. From a brightly antiseptic world that had enclosed him and maintained him in drugged contentment, he has escaped to no more than the chill of approaching night. A choir lets rip on the soundtrack to cheer his spirits, but something stronger is needed for the rest of us.

poses a problem to the organizers of the world's most violent sport, designed to entertain the populace of the year 2018 now that such diversions as poverty, sickness and war have been abolished. The moral of the game is that individual effort counts for nothing, but Caan subverts this by surviving one bloody contest after another and becoming a popular hero. Since his heroics are confined to the track, while for the other two-thirds of the film he merely comes over as inarticulate and dull, the film is vaguely worrying rather than convincing – worrying because the game of Rollerball is genuinely exciting and demonstrably

Perhaps the unsatisfactory nature of both Montag and Thex is that they are followers rather than leaders – a more dynamic outlaw is called for. In *Sleeper* (1973), he's Woody Allen, waking up two hundred years after a minor ulcer operation to find himself in demand as a Resistance leader against the totalitarian world state. Briefly and hilariously disguised as a domestic robot, he achieves fame by kidnapping a nose, all that remains of the dictator; but when challenged to produce his own formula for a stable society he has nothing more enterprising to offer than sex and death. In Norman Jewison's *Rollerball* (1975) based on William Harrison's hypnotic short story, the dynamism of James Caan

futile, emasculating us all into the role of spectators. The politics of the future would surely call for more sense and less carnage.

In Barry Shear's *Wild in the Streets* (1968), by contrast, the new Messiah is a young pop singer who decides that government is no longer safe or suitable in the hands of the middle aged or elderly, and gets himself elected as President. He promptly institutes compulsory retirement at the age of 30 and 'Retirement Homes' – where everyone is forcibly fed on LSD – for all citizens over 35. America abandons international affairs, except that her wealth is generously shared out to less fortunate nations, and she becomes a land of drugged and dreaming idlers. The President, a contented family man, has only one steadily growing problem: a recalcitrant younger generation that is determined to put everyone out of business over the age of 10.

The film is uneven, but with a nice line in comedy, depending on quick, bitter gags occasionally worthy of the Marx Brothers. There are good performances, too, from Shelley Winters, Christopher Jones and the unnerving Diane Varsi. It's certainly vastly preferable to *Privilege* (1967), in which pop-idol Paul Jones is used by the Government to keep the country manageable. Performances in which he is handcuffed, beaten up and caged by sadistic police officers are seen as a way of confining the energies of British youth to harmless and controlled rioting. Jones, for one, finds this an unconvincing theory and finally revolts against it, encouraged by Jean Shrimpton. Rather as with Thex, the only effect his revolt has is to put him out in the cold. 'Privilege must not be misused to disturb the public mind,' concludes Peter Watkins's commentary, in mock-quotation from an official communiqué.

·Watkins is a specialist in the television-verité style, whereby the participants in the events he's staging respond solemnly to questions from an unseen interviewer. It's a technique with substantial emotive force, but Watkins usually undermines it by being less than explicit about the events themselves, as in *The Peace Game* (1969) which suggested that warfare will soon be replaced by controlled bouts of aggression between small groups of representative soldiers under the guidance of a computer. Watkins displays great indignation about this unlikely device – which is a little perverse of him in that he invented it – but it's difficult to share his indignation since the game apparently leads nowhere and bores the hide off its spectators. He was in better shape with *Punishment Park* (1971), in which draft-dodgers, demonstrators and other undesirable youth elements who refuse to take part in the war in Indo-China are allowed to choose between prison and a three-day session in the desert avoiding capture by an assault force of troops and police. Following one such group, the film shows them being picked off one by one, in growing horror and desperation; as in the final images of *Peace Game*, the troops close in at the end with lethal truncheons while Watkins's voice (he's the detached observer, as usual) screams at them to stop.

It's a troublesome piece of work, largely because while Watkins's sincerity is never in doubt one can't help thinking the case could be rendered more watertight. Fact works more potently when presented as fiction than fiction clothed as documentary. This is partly because the audience agrees with it more easily ('it *could* happen, you know') instead of being inclined to argue ('it *would* never happen like that'). There is strangely more truth in the mythic fantasy of *Night of the Living Dead* than in the apparent realities of *Punishment Park*. And, for that matter, more truth in *Seven Days in May* (1964), which begins with demonstrators outside the White House, clashing inconclusively over the President's disarmament pact with Russia, and moves into the Pentagon to show the fight continuing at the highest level and with the utmost secrecy. Scripted by Rod Serling and directed in goldfish-bowl surroundings by John Frankenheimer, it sprang recognizably from the same fears as *Manchurian Candidate* but was played solid and straight by Fredric March, Burt Lancaster and Kirk Douglas, with Ava Gardner beachcombing once again in the background.

Fantasies about changes in leadership are infrequent in the cinema, not least because they can be suspected of casting doubts on the existing régime. But retrospective fables come easier, like *Bormann* (1968), an Italian/French extravaganza in which the Nazi leader plots the overthrow of mankind with a new super-race, or the Czech film *I, Justice* (1968), which supposes that Hitler himself has survived the war, held captive by a group of men determined to exact an adequate revenge from him for his crimes. In doing so, they end up as neo-fascists, spreading a new tide of wholesale murder. Slightly too elaborate, for its own good, the film was directed with spectacular authority by Zbynek Brynych, and deserves to be better known, as does that other fantasy of political disquiet, Theodore Flicker's *The President's Analyst* (1968), in which James Coburn has to monitor the behaviour of President James Gregory (of *Manchurian Candidate* fame) and quickly sails off round the bend under the pressure of sharing responsibility for several million people.

The attempt to control the uncontrollable sets up most of the tensions of 'utopian' films, which reflect, like history, a zig-zag progression between anarchy and dictatorship, propelled by issues of the day like pollution, overpopulation or conservation. In Steven Spielberg's *Los Angeles 2017* (1970), adapted from the novel by Philip Wylie, it was a case of underground survival after Los Angeles (and just about everywhere else) has been killed off by smog. Gene Barry is invited to join the team of 'resistants' who don't like having to take anti-reactive pills and being ordered around by Barry Sullivan; they want to go to the surface again and take their chances with the smog. Barry finds at the end that it was all a dream, but he looks Very Thoughtful. The film's chief interest is that Spielberg, later to make *Duel, Sugarland Express* and *Jaws*, was even at this stage finding plenty to say about the hermetic world of the car interior.

Smog descended again in *Zero Population Growth* (1971), in which the fresh-air fiend was once more the

(right) Anti-war demonstrators are submitted to the violence of *Punishment Park* (Francoise Films and Chartwell Films, 1971).

man who kept his windows closed; wearing filter-masks, people had to queue for hours just to admire small plots of synthetic grass. The Government has decided that no child is to be born for the next 30 years, and offenders will receive the death penalty; the offenders in this case are Oliver Reed and Geraldine Chaplin, tired of making do with walkie-talkie dolls. The same idea, with similar lack of impact, came in the same year with *The Last Child*, in which Van Heflin and Janet Margolin grappled with the authorities, while the German production *I Love You, I Kill You* (1971) had a benevolent police force handing out birth-control pills. More fun was to be had with *Curious Female* (1969), in which love and family life are frowned upon and as a consequence the showing of

Rouge, except for one five-year-old who will have to be impregnated if the world is to survive.

Nevertheless, it's the spectre of a world too crowded to live on that haunts the science-fiction writers most obsessively, and with *Soylent Green* (1973), Richard Fleischer brought Harry Harrison's memorable novel *Make Room! Make Room!* at long last to the screen (it was written in 1966) to reveal New York suffocating beneath a population of forty million in the year 2022. Although murders in this environment are not only frequent but welcome, a police force still exists and one of its members is Charlton Heston; he gets his teeth into an out-of-the-ordinary killing, and in following up the clues he discovers the secret of the synthetic foods that are supplied by the giant Soylent company.

20th-century movies is illegal (as may yet prove to be the case during the current decade).

At the other end of the scale are those pleasingly nonsensical films in which the problem is *under-population*: an example is *Captive Women* (1952), in which a bashful Ron Randell finds himself in New York in 3000 AD, where the Mutates pursue the Norms in hope of spawning a decent plot. In *Terror from the Year 5000* (1956), a machine that can obtain objects from the future secures a mutant lady on the hunt for men to restock the human race, aided by her unusual talent for hypnotizing people with a wave of her fingernails. And in *Crimes of the Future* (1970), an inventively scurrilous film by the unclassifiable David Cronenberg, all post-pubertal females have died of a disease invented by the mad dermatologist Antoine

(above) Alex (Malcolm McDowell) and his gang of Droogs in the Korova Milkbar (with special sculptures by Herman Makkink in *A Clockwork Orange* (Warners, 1971).

The added protein is being derived from human corpses, fresh from the euthanasia clinics where people are encouraged to depart this life in comfort and tranquillity.

Although the crowd scenes are given an acceptable measure of claustrophobia, with bodies being shovelled about like compost by riot-control vehicles rather implausibly resembling tractors, *Soylent Green* misses too many opportunities for its own good, paying only distant attention to the special effects that Fleischer made such a feature of in *Fantastic Voyage*. When Heston passes on his terrible secret to Brook Peters at the end, it is difficult to decide whether he is hero or fool; cannibalism seems a logical resort under the circumstances, and the process is maintained with discreet efficiency. And the film simply isn't convincing enough for one to care too much either way. What it *does* represent, fortuitously, is the passing of an era by showing us the 'death' of Edward G. Robinson, placidly making his farewell to the strains of Beethoven's Pastoral Symphony. For this sequence at least, we can believe that a measure of dignity and individuality have departed from the world and only the locusts are left.

Bodies littered the streets again in Liliana Cavani's *Year of the Cannibals* (1971), in which the story of Antigone is updated to a period after World War III. They are the corpses of insurgents against the Government and they are left in the Milan streets to rot as a lesson to other would-be revolutionaries. Britt Ekland isn't inclined to leave her brother's body outside a coffee-bar, so she enlists famed insurgent Pierre Clementi to help with the burial, disregarding the death penalty for such an act. For a while they drift about in a fetchingly unclothed condition, which makes it easy for the police to trace them and administer the standard brutalities. Despite the allegiances to Sophocles, the film does little more than look occasionally striking and is of interest more as a preparation for the heightened masochism of *Night Porter* than as science fiction, but it illustrates once more the chances afforded by the genre for incongruity.

It's all too seldom that the irreconcilable factions of the future are shown to settle their differences, to clear away the bodies, acknowledge all mistakes, share all confidences. In *Metropolis*, the Master of the city and his shuffling shop-floor steward manage, haltingly, that slate-wiping handshake, although you wouldn't trust either of them beyond the end credits. And in *Clockwork Orange* (1971) the prole and his inquisitors agree to wipe out the brainwashing that has become a matter of some inconvenience to both of them. In answer to the hordes of movies that have ended with the battle-lines still drawn, with Thex and Montag in melancholy exile, *A Clockwork Orange* affirms that totalitarianism is a state of mind, not a state of nature – nor even a state of grace.

'The attempt to impose upon man, a creature of growth and capable of sweetness, to ooze juicily at the last round the bearded lips of God, to attempt to impose, I say, laws and conditions appropriate to a mechanical creation, against this I raise my sword-pen.' Having satirized his theme in this manner, Anthony Burgess felt free to expound it in a fresh and thoroughly unconventional disguise in his book. It's the story of Alex DeLarge who, in a future no great distance from now, is imprisoned for murder, rehabilitated by aversion therapy, and restored hastily to his former self when the side effects of the rehabilitation drive him to attempt suicide and the popular press rushes to his support. His reign of terror given new respectability,

he is even more potent than before.

Stepping out from the shadow of *2001*, which would have typecast a lesser director for life, Kubrick demonstrates with *A Clockwork Orange* the skill with which he can structure a simple conversation piece in a simple domestic setting, extract perfect timing from his actors, select lighting and lenses with invincible authority, and edit his material ruthlessly to achieve an unflagging pace. His film is boisterous, intimate, explicit and gaudy, owing nothing to the aseptic architectures of *2001*. The exteriors are glassy, box-like, and cluttered with rubbish; the interiors are lurid, inelegant and uneasily angular with contemporary furniture that looks like tomorrow's suburban left-overs. Inhabiting these inhospitable cells are the ageing exponents of today's fashions, locked as though ice-bound into their trendy gear.

Against these miraculous settings, the film bursts with energy; movement is a vital part of each scene, a torrential, dancing flow. The superb fight sequence quickly establishes the mood, as the gangs confront each other gleefully in a ballet of dazzling violence, hurling themselves through furniture and windows with slapstick enthusiasm. Urged on by, and often synchronized with, the thundering music of Rossini, their exhilaration then bursts out into a headlong car-ride through the night, scattering other traffic in wild panic and yelling with the sheer joy of speed. At their head, Malcolm McDowell is ideal as Alex, whether required to fling his recalcitrant gang into the river in slow motion, cringe resentfully from authority, or face in growing horror the realization that everything he values most in life is going to turn his stomach from now on. His tortured face, encompassed by straps and wires, his eyelids held open by vicious clamps, is one of the most haunting sights in science fiction cinema.

At the centre of all Kubrick's films is an endurance test, and *Clockwork Orange* continues the pattern. Alex sets in motion an inescapable retribution, culminating in his suicide attempt as a result of the allergy his treatment has given him to Beethoven's Ninth. Then, like Bowman in *2001*, he is reborn ('I came back to life after black, black night for what might have been a million years'), and is carefully restored to his original anarchism by attentive specialists. Winston Smith never had it so good. His new wisdom gives him a tremendous, if unspecified power which he can be expected to devote to self-indulgence; the parallels to *2001* seem too clearly pointed to be accidental, not least the opening shot of *A Clockwork Orange* in which the Starchild's unblinking gaze can be seen in the stare Alex gives us as the camera retreats from his face to the other side of the room.

There is an awareness of potency in that look, a sense of power that will be wielded not wisely but too well. The end of the world as we know it is in his eyes.

Yet I do seriously, and upon good Grounds, affirm it possible to make a Flying Chariot, in which a man may sit, and give such motion unto it, as shall convey him through the Air. And this perhaps might be made large enough to carry Divers men at the same time, together with Food for their Viaticum, and Commodities for Traffique. So that notwithstanding all these seeming impossibilities, 'tis likely enough, that there may be means invented of Journeying to the Moone. And how happy they shall be that are first successful in this attempt!
Bishop Wilkins.

TAKING OFF

(previous pages) Sir Cedric Hardwicke leaves the ground in the film of Jules Verne's first tale of exploration, *Five Weeks in a Balloon* (Fox, 1962).

First flights: (left) Hans Albers and Sybille Schmitz in Karl Hartl's *FPI Doesn't Answer* (Gaumont/Fox/UFA, 1933). (right) Ernst Fegté's lunar surface, Bonestell's backdrop, and Heinlein's characters, plus some remarkably cumbersome hardware, in *Destination Moon* (Eagle-Lion, 1950).

The image that dominates science fiction is that of the rocket, a projectile bearing many meanings and subject to endless variations of design. When Verne first considered the subject in the 1860s, placing the launch-pad remarkably close to Cape Kennedy, he packed off his space-travellers in a giant bullet unleashed from a cannon. The military implications were unavoidable: a rocket could carry explosives as easily as people, it was capable of travelling immense distances, and it could come down with as much speed as it could go up. Whether its purpose was to be for exploration or for destruction, it was the symbol of the future. Taking due heed, the future used it for both.

Two other influences contributed to its shape – the airship and the submarine, slowly making headway into reality from the speculative pages of the popular magazines of the 1880s. They had wings, propellors, sails, balloons, turrets, flags and anchors, and resembled everything from whales to Chinese fireworks; in silhouette, they sometimes even looked like flying saucers. For a while, the cinema made the same connections, and a weird assortment of spacecraft came off the Méliès assembly line, but after Lang had consulted with the experts Hermann Oberth and Willy Ley in 1929 there was considerable streamlining, and the tapering cylinder became traditional. Ironically, the science-fiction magazines of the period found that their readership responded better to the baroque and the colourful, and their skies were accordingly filled with corrugated spaceliners, peppered with portholes; the trend continues with today's paperbacks and the asymmetrical pin-cushions of Chris Foss, but it took *2001* (doubtless under Arthur Clarke's influence) to convince the film-makers that a spaceship travels at the same speed no matter how it's shaped, so long as it doesn't have to contend with an atmosphere.

Quaintly anachronistic reconstructions of Verne would have to wait until the appropriate mood of nostalgia bestowed an affectionate gaze on such adventures as *Around the World in Eighty Days* (1956) or *Five Weeks in a Balloon* (1962). In the '30s, dodging round a miscellany of depressions, a speedy departure to better worlds seemed advisable, and so there were new and enterprising designs for flight in such films as *Just Imagine* (1930), *Sky High* (1931), and Karl Hartl's *FPI Doesn't Answer* (1933), which suggested a floating aerodrome in mid-Atlantic. Balanced on compressed air tanks, the platform was sunk by saboteurs after some dramatic scenes of tri-motor planes landing and taking off; the concept itself was sunk by enormous flying wings of *Things to Come* (1936), growling down out of the clouds to consolidate a new era of air-power. By the following year, uninterrupted transatlantic flight seemed wholly plausible in *Non-Stop New York*, while the ultra-modern aeroplane, The Wing, was being flown against the serial hero in *Dick Tracy*. It was also the time of *Lost Horizon* (1936), whose plot makes a fascinating counterpoint to the concluding moments of *Things to Come*; as the 1,500-foot Space Gun hurls the young lovers on their way to the Moon and Cabal demands that the choice be made between 'the universe or nothingness, Passworthy', Ronald Colman struggles back towards Shangri-La and the prospect of eternal life. The universe, perhaps, can wait awhile.

Given the events of the following ten years, it was a wise decision. Too many terrestrial horizons were lost for the cinema's sights to be raised very far from ground level. But when the nothingness had been averted, the universe called once more, and the rocket-men applied their new skills to less mundane targets than the suburbs of London. Cheered on by the science-fiction fans, the space race received its starting signal from *Destination*

Moon in 1950. Directed by Irving Pichel, the film was derived from Heinlein's juvenile novel *Rocket Ship Galileo* (1947) about a group of boys who build their own spaceship, go to the Moon and foil a Nazi plot being hatched there. Traces of this ingenuous fantasy remained in George Pal's production: the characters are one-dimensional, quick with self-sacrifice, slapstick humour and quiet pride, and they are sent on their way by private enterprise, having informed the richest men in America that 'we're not the only ones who are trying to reach the Moon – the first country that can control the Moon with missiles can control the Earth'.

The adventure is fraught with difficulties that are now routine but which were breathtakingly new to general audiences at the time; the take-off is a noisy affair complete with distorted faces, one of the crew drifts off during a spacewalk and has to be rescued, and there isn't quite enough fuel at the end to get everybody home again. On the whole, it was an accurate rendering of popular science fiction and a remarkable picture of science fact, thanks to the guidance of rocket-expert Hermann Oberth, brilliant space-artist Chesley Bonestell,

and Heinlein himself who managed to keep the plot free of 'a version of the script which included dude ranches, cowboys, guitars and hillbilly songs on the Moon, plus a trio of female hepsters singing into a mike'. With *Destination Moon* space-flight ceased to be the exclusive province of Flash Gordon and became a legitimate patriotic enterprise – in time even Abbott and Costello and the Miss Universe Contest Beauties went into orbit.

Before investigating the cinema's discoveries on other planets, a quick look is in order at the films which stayed close to home, acting partly as commentary on the progress of the space programme and partly as an alarmist reflection of what could go wrong with those foolish enough to make giant leaps for mankind. Amid the blizzard of trips to the Moon, Mars and Venus, there were a number of reminders that it wasn't going to be so easy – films like *The Quatermass Xperiment* (1954) and *The First Man into Space* (1959), in which the pioneers returned in hideous disarray. There were warnings that the first signs of extra-planetary activity would bring reprisals from alien observers, who would use everything from Martian heat-rays to mind-control to make us change our minds; by the time of *Cape Canaveral Monsters* (1960), it was plain that the officials who attempted to foil the *Destination Moon* take-off were not only Communists but Zombies controlled from the stratosphere. In more subtle discouragement, rocket crews seemed to be riddled with neuroses, as in *Riders to the Stars* (1953), which had its disgruntled astronauts chasing meteorites, or *Spaceways* (1953), in which Howard Duff had to prove he hadn't murdered his wife and put her body in a satellite. In *Satellite in the Sky* (1956), Kieron Moore and Donald Wolfit had to work out how to prevent a space-bomb from demolishing the people who placed it in orbit; human sacrifice turned out to be the only answer.

David Lean's *The Sound Barrier* (1952) brilliantly captured the contradictory moods of the period with its demonstration that the new technology was being steered by the same grim determination that Britain had shown during the war, and that a similarly heavy price would have to be paid. In less restrained terms, *The Flame Barrier* (1958) saw would-be satellites returned scorchingly to earth wrapped in red-hot living protoplasm (a reminder of the fashion in the magazines at one time for stories of malevolent communities hanging around in the clouds). In real life the Apollo programme went ahead regardless, urged on by a generation raised on Heinlein, Clarke, Van Vogt and Bradbury, whose story *Icarus Montgolfier Wright*, transferred glowingly to the screen through the eerie nostalgia of Joe Mugnaini's artwork, won itself an Oscar nomination in 1962. It was a prose poem to the rocket and the men who made it possible, and it told them that all the dangers and deaths had been worthwhile.

Optimism and disenchantment continued to war

Emergencies in space (right and far right) Richard Jaeckel trains his blaster on samples of *The Green Slime* (MGM, 1968), while (above) David Janssen arrives too late to save the pilot of Ironman One in *Marooned* (Columbia, 1969).

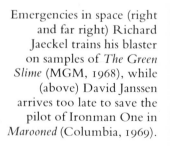

during the 1960s, with Bradbury finally losing to Malzberg when it was confirmed that the Moon had little to offer visually or geologically and the public began to wonder how else their money could be spent. Signposting this uneasiness was *Marooned* (1969), a big, glossy and absorbing production directed with neutral efficiency by John Sturges (of *Magnificent Seven* fame). Richard Crenna, James Franciscus and Gene Hackman get stuck in orbit when their retro-rockets fail, and Gregory Peck, the eyes of the President and the world upon him, has to get them back. Thanks to the Russians, and despite an untimely hurricane, he manages to save two out of three by looking serious and talking into microphones, but not before everybody has had a good chance to wonder what this bunch of jittering neurotics (Hackman is particularly unmanageable) is doing there in the first place. There are some oddities in the special effects – the Russian arrives in what looks like a hand-grenade – but the film has a pleasingly ironic edge. 'Let's do this scientifically,' suggests one of the astronauts when the news sinks in that somebody will have to go. 'The two big guys throw the little guy out, OK?'

Suspension in space seems to bring out the worst in people. In Tom Gries's *Earth II* (1971), a Chinese missile hovering over Moscow gets Mariette Hartley in such a state (she has a bad enough time as Hackman's wife in *Marooned*) that she sends it off towards the sun from her husband's space-station; to be honest, she miscalculates slightly, and it heads towards Earth instead, but there's a gratifying amount of panic even if one suspects Gries can do better things. In *War Between the Planets* (1966), everybody on the Gamma One space-station is jumpy through overwork and the arrival of an asteroid threat to the Earth doesn't help matters; bombs are detonated all over the place before (as in *Earth II*) space can be declared clean for the younger generation. The younger generation doesn't derive much benefit; on satellite Gamma Three, the remains of another rogue asteroid turn out to include *The Green Slime* (1968), which multiplies into a whole army of trundling freaks, bright-eyed, tentacular, and undoubtedly green and slimy. Featuring Robert Horton and Luciana Paluzzi under the direction of Kinji Fukasaku, this curiously hybrid production has stoical American astronauts dashing about and grimacing in unison like the peasants in Kurosawa films.

The only problem Verne's astronauts had was how to replenish their stocks of wine, so when Méliès made the cinema's first Moon-trip he embroidered the story with Selenites taken from Wells's *First Men on the Moon*. They were spiky and athletic types, conveniently exploding when tapped sharply with an umbrella; the Baltimore Gun Club adventurers were able to escape far more easily than the luckless Cavor, and the *Trip to the Moon* (1902) was completed when the sheer pull of gravity drew the projectile back to Earth. Wells received more respectful treatment in 1919, with the

first British production of *First Men on the Moon*, in which Hector Abbas and Lionel D'Aragon arrive by pumpkin-like capsule and meet a Grand Lunar with a huge white head. In Nathan Juran's rather boring 1964 version Lionel Jeffries comically heads the expedition in a golfball protected with railway buffers and meets a lunar race that turns to stone in times of eclipse.

Although his balloon and submarine stories have had a successful screen career, Verne's flights into space have

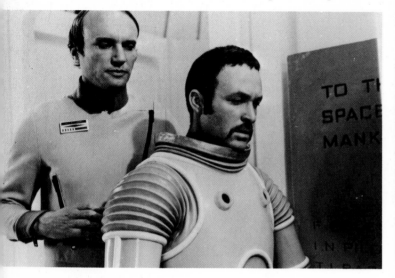

been disappointingly handled. Byron Haskin brought style but stifling sobriety to *From the Earth to the Moon* (1958), in which Joseph Cotten sent George Sanders and Debra Paget on their uneventful trip, while Don Sharp went to the other extreme with *Jules Verne's Rocket to the Moon* (1967) in which, thanks to the clowning of Terry-Thomas, Hermione Gingold, Graham Stark, Lionel Jeffries and others, the story barely managed to leave the ground. Perhaps the film that came closest to Verne in spirit was in fact Fritz Lang's *Frau im Mond* (1929), written by Lang and his wife Thea von Harbou with painstaking attention to scientific detail but with an anaemic story in which the astronauts (in everyday clothes) wander the lunar surface collecting gold and raw diamonds. The photography, which incorporated work by the trail-blazing animator Oskar Fischinger, put *Metropolis* to shame – but nothing else did.

With the exception of *Destination Moon*, films about our nearest neighbour seemed to demonstrate only too clearly that the aliens were right to discourage us, for our own good. In 1953, Heinlein contributed another screenplay in the form of *Project Moonbase*, which has been allowed quietly to drop from sight; directed by Richard Talmadge, it crashed an exploring rocket on to the lunar surface, with two survivors, a man and a woman (called, as only Heinlein could call her, Colonel Brighteyes). Doomed, they are married long-distance by the female US President. It sounds magnificent, and so does *Cat-Women of the Moon* (1953), filmed in 3D,

which revealed the centre of the planet to be tenanted by telepathic cat-ladies and giant spiders – a story so memorable that they filmed it again in 1958 as *Missile to the Moon*, adding some gangsters and rock-creatures for good measure.

In *Twelve to the Moon* (1960), the Selenites react unfavourably to a landing on the Menelaus crater by spraying the Earth with an icy white cloud. This was followed up with virulent fungus in *Mutiny in Outer Space* (1964), which gives the astronauts a dose of 'space raptures' until they hit on the idea of killing it off with artificial sub-zero particles, one of those instant cures of which the advertisements always speak so well. By the time of *Countdown* (1967), the inventive pace has begun to flag, and Robert Altman plays it straight with a race to beat the Russians to the Moon-landing.

(far left) James Olson and Ori Levy in Roy Baker's *Moon Zero Two* (Hammer/Warners, 1969). (left) Yulia Salontsena as the Queen of Mars in Protazanov's *Aelita* (Mezhrobpom, 1924). (above) A Danish crew reaches Mars in *The Sky Ship* (Nordisk, 1917).

James Caan and Robert Duvall (teamed here long before their *Godfather* partnership) make an edgy American crew, surrounded by good authentic sets – although their story had lost thirty minutes by the time it reached Britain and consequently became a little obscure at times. Some obscurity would probably have helped *Mission Stardust* (1968), based on the Perry Rhodan stories by Walter Ernsting; when a private spaceship arrives on the Moon, it discovers Essy Persson, a beautiful alien with time on her hands. Released at the same time as *Barbarella*, it had the right ideas but far too few of them. All that remained was for *Moon Zero Two* (1969) to turn the Moon into a frontier town, brawling with gunplay, prospectors and tourists, for the Selenites to emigrate in the direction of Andromeda. We shall not see their like again.

The next area for colonization, of course, was the planet Mars, containing better prospects for being inhabited thanks to those canals and subtle colour changes. First audiences for *A Trip to Mars* (1902) must have found it familiar, the Méliès *Trip to the Moon* having been copied and the title changed by competitors in the States. When Edwin S. Porter made a genuine *Trip to Mars* in 1910 it was something of a horror film: a gigantic demon captured the Earthman wandering on his nose, turned him into a snowball and flung him back to Earth on a puff of wind. A more inspirational visit was made by the Danish crew of Holger-Madsen's *Sky Ship* (1917), whose quaint propeller-driven craft conveyed them in no time to a stern Druidical civilization with a philosophy of peace and love, a beach-ball globe of the Earth to prove their point, and a remarkable floor-show of dancing maidens. More surprises were in store with the Russian film *Aelita* (1924), derived from Tolstoy by Jacob Protazanov. The Queen of Mars, her chunky palace hung, drawn and quartered with bits of scaffolding and piano-wire, falls in love with the young Russian she can observe on Earth with the Martian equivalent of a *camera obscura*. Fortunately he is to be the first cosmonaut and he is soon overthrowing the unsavoury Martian social structure in favour of something closer to what the folks have got back home. Full of zest and humour, and given bizarre perspectives by its expressionist sets, *Aelita* contains as much Flash Gordon as Tolstoy and deserves to be better known. David Butler's *Just Imagine* (1930), a science-fiction musical comedy, was more conservative when it got as far as the Martian surface, where the corn grew high and the struggle between good and evil was still in evidence.

(left and below) Paul Mantee in Death Valley as Byron Haskin's castaway, *Robinson Crusoe on Mars* (Paramount, 1964).
(opposite) The occupants of Ironman One in *Marooned* (Columbia, 1969). Gene Hackman reads while James Franciscus gets his daily exercise.

Again, Mars was left unattended for a while until *Destination Moon* established that space travel was good box-office. Then came *Rocketship XM* (1950), a quickly shot film by Kurt Neumann which rushed its crew to Mars in mountaineering outfits to find that the planet has been ravaged by atomic war and only purple mutants are left. More amenable was Marguerite Chapman, called Alita after Tolstoy, discovered under the Martian sands by Cameron Mitchell in *Flight to Mars* (1951). She seems to have put George Pal off his stride when he set out to repeat his *Destination Moon* success with a film of the Willy Ley/Chesley Bonestell book *The Conquest of Space* (1955), which actually derived more from Werner von Braun's *The Mars Project* filtered through screenplay-writers Philip Yordan and Barré Lyndon. Directed by Byron Haskin, *Conquest of Space* acquired (as his *War of the Worlds* had done) a curious religious undertone, but it was technically superb to watch – as good as the later NASA documentaries. It presented Mars, however, as a young and potentially verdant planet, an error that Haskin was at pains to correct when he made *Robinson Crusoe on Mars* in 1964.

By contrast with the Moon, Mars seems to have found film-makers in generally respectful mood, as though the poetic fantasies of Bradbury's *Martian Chronicles* had made a lasting impression of fragile and dignified antiquity. Haskin's *Robinson Crusoe on Mars*, tactfully, sensibly and convincingly staged in the bleak hostility of California's Death Valley, is one of the best science-fiction movies ever made on the problems of being cast adrift on a desert planet. The idea (and the alien called Friday) is taken from Defoe, but the technicalities of survival come from hard science and they are fascinating to observe. As always with Haskin, the colours have a texture of their own, and the photography is a delight, rising brilliantly to the challenge of the final sequences in which, providentially, a volcano erupts at the Martian ice-cap and the US Navy spaceship arrives to the rescue. Science-fiction movies have to work harder than most to appear plausible, but *Robinson Crusoe on Mars*, monkey and all, is a notable triumph, leaving little room for doubt that it would happen exactly like this.

Science fiction without its Martians would also be

(left) A scene from Kubrick's superb epic *2001: A Space Odyssey* (MGM, 1968).
(above) The surface of Venus as pictured by the Russians in *Planet of Storms* (Sovexportfilm, 1962).

the poorer, and the cinema has come up with some extraordinary specimens ranging from the muscle-bound reptilian in *It! The Terror from Beyond Space* (1958) to Tommy Kirk as a Martian hunting for a mate in *Mars Needs Women* (1966). Curtis Harrington's *Queen of Blood* (1966) features Florence Marly as a blood-sucking, egg-laying alien, studied in disbelief by such distinguished admirers as Basil Rathbone and Forrest J. Ackerman. This was a Corman production, by the way, made at a time when several Russian science-fiction films had been bought for American distribution and were used to make a whole library of backgrounds and stock-shots. The source for *Queen of Blood* is unidentifiable, but Corman's *Battle Beyond the Sun* (1963) took its Mars-scapes from *The Heavens*

Call (1959), in which a Russian team rescues an American expedition stranded on Mars.

The Russian production that seems to have provided the greatest amount of this kind of mileage was *Planet of Storms*, directed by Pavel Klushantsev in 1962. Also known as *Cosmonauts on Venus*, it featured some spectacular landscapes, a jovial robot, and a number of malignant dinosaurs and other life-forms. The human element was far from outstanding, but Corman quickly changed all that; he gave the material to John Sebastian and Stephanie Rothman (of *Student Nurses* fame) and issued the result under the title *Voyage to the Prehistoric Planet* (1965), starring Basil Rathbone and Faith Domergue. He then recruited Peter Bogdanovich (of *Last Picture Show* fame) to get to work on what was left, and the result appeared in 1968 under the title *Voyage to the Planet of Prehistoric Women*; it starred Mamie Van Doren as a telepathic amphibian native Venerian in sea-shell bra, and it's not the sort of thing you see too often, even though it also masqueraded under the titles *Gill Woman* and *Gill Women of Venus*. It should not be confused, however, with *Women of the*

Prehistoric Planet (1965), directed by Arthur Pierce, which is an – er – original, in which Wendell Corey has trouble with Centaurians on a primitive planet resembling a small greenhouse.

Otherwise, Venus has been strangely neglected, apart from the East German/Polish production *First Spaceship on Venus* (1959) which starred Yoko Tani and was based on Stanislaw Lem's first science-fiction novel *The Astronauts*. Disliked by Lem himself, it nevertheless sounds promising to admirers of *Solaris*; the story is of an expedition from a Utopian and classless Earth to the surface of Venus, where they discover the planet has been laid waste by atomic warfare. It couldn't have been worse than *Zontar: the Thing from Venus* (1966), an uncredited remake of *It Conquered the World*, in which John Agar struggles wearily with a large telepathic bat that insists on telling Earthmen how to behave.

It has taken Ray Bradbury, a specialist in Martian affairs, to provide one of the most memorable pictures of Venus, brought effectively to life by Jack Smight in one of the three episodes of *The Illustrated Man* (1968). A rocket-ship crew has crash-landed on the planet, where the rain is an unending torrent, and they must now struggle through the downpour to reach the shelter of the sun-dome, a geodesic refuge boasting every comfort. One by one, the crew members prove to be a washout – one man drowns himself simply by looking up at the sky – and only Rod Steiger makes it to the dome where Claire Bloom (a great improvement on Bradbury's hot chocolate with marshmallow dollops) is waiting for him. Set in a scrubby no-man's land of inhospitable countryside, *The Illustrated Man* has a uniquely alien quality throughout, although only its Venus episode is overtly extraterrestrial. The other two are *The Veldt* (about children who turn their nursery into a death-trap for parents) and *The Last Night of the World* (in which parents are ordered to kill their children to escape the imminent ordeal of the end of the world). These are among the stories to be found on the 'skin illustrations' that cover Steiger from head to foot (more or less); his obsession with the lady who put them there is expanded by the film in leisurely detail, so that when the stories come to life they appear logically enough to stem from the central tension between the enigmatic artist and her animated canvas. The link is reinforced by the re-appearance of the same actors in each tale and in roughly the same roles.

The unwary astronaut occasionally travels farther in time than in space and finds himself not having left the planet at all. In 1955, Hugh Marlowe aims for Mars in *World Without End* and thanks to a time warp he lands on Earth in 2508 AD where Rod Taylor needs help against the mutants, giant spiders and other menacing occupants of the world's atomic-infected surface. In Edgar G. Ulmer's *Beyond the Time Barrier* (1960), the story is much the same, with Robert Clarke flying into 2024 AD to discover a power struggle between surface

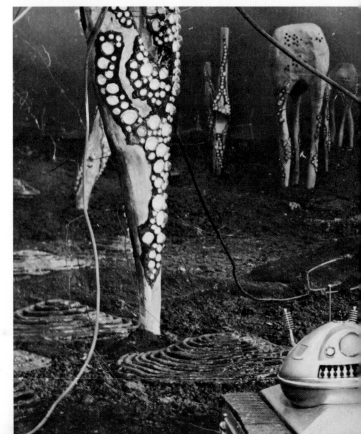

and underground communities. So it's not too much of a surprise when the Statue of Liberty comes into view in *Planet of the Apes* (1967); rather, since the parallels between ape and human behaviour have been established throughout the film, it's a surprise they didn't admit to it earlier.

Having dwindled through four sequels to an abominable television series, the original *Planet of the Apes* risks being mislaid among the imitations as nothing more than the one that started it all. In fact it remains very much more, a cool demonstration of film-making beside which the sequels look like comic-strips. Franklin Schaffner dealt with the manipulations of politics in *The Best Man* and the raw poetry of primitivism in *The War Lord*, and the two themes flow together for *Planet of the Apes* and onward to *Patton* where George C. Scott takes over the Charlton Heston role as the growling, self-opinionated leader attempting to apply his own code at odds with the temper of the times. The apes, scrupulously following their own laws, are startled to find this arrogant relic in their midst, asserting what is manifestly untrue – that he and his kind are their superiors – and finally they cast him out to come to his senses. With all respect to Paul Dehn's careful scripts for *Beneath the Planet of the Apes* (1969), *Escape from* (1971), and *Conquest of* (1972), the introduction of mutant humans lurking in the ruins of New York, the time-switch that brings three apes back to the 'present', or the rebellion that the apes stage against their servile status – these are merely devices that obscure the clean lines of the original. The 'final' film, *Battle for the Planet of the Apes* (1973), adds John Huston to the ape cast but is otherwise intolerably short of ideas for ape activity and has only the whisper of a statement to make about racism – a statement which in any case is hardly at its most effective in the ape context.

The script for *Planet of the Apes* was by the late Rod Serling, derived from Pierre Boulle's *Monkey Planet*, but words were not the strength of Schaffner's film. It is, rather, a magnificent visual experience, from the emerald lake at the beginning to the ominous sea-shore at the close. The desolate landscapes of the Utah and Arizona National Parks, parched and sculpted into primeval ruins, make an appropriately unearthly setting for the first appearance of the apes, black and shining like stormtroopers, rounding up humans like cattle. And if the ape town is disappointingly shapeless, the interiors less comfortable than one would expect, the apes themselves remain astonishing successes of make-up and performance. As with *The War Lord*,

(above) Rod Steiger and Claire Bloom as the troubled parents in a story from *The Illustrated Man* (Warners, 1968). (left) an East European picture of *The First Spaceship on Venus* (Defa and Film Polski, 1959), also known as *The Silent Planet* and adapted from a story by Stanislaw Lem.

Schaffner has created a new world from the dislocations of the old; like Bradbury's Mars, it is haunted with familiarities rendered suddenly strange and unmanageable, and like the other planets in the solar system it finds human beings something of an embarrassment.

On the other hand, the new worlds of Stanley Kubrick are familiar, if at all, only to science-fiction fans, some of whom, over-reacting to the perfections of *2001: A Space Odyssey* (1968), asserted grumpily that it was thirty years out of date. What undermines the film's whole theory of man's dependence on otherworldly forces, however, is nothing to do with the repetition of a traditional science-fiction concept; it is, simply, the film's own existence. As Arthur Clarke stated, if any space-travel film is going to be better than *2001* it will have to be made on location. With a battery of special effects designed by Kubrick himself, the universe has been astonishingly recreated and populated. No strings, no visible backdrops, and just a few, almost indistinguishable touches of process work. With his multi-million dollar investment, the entire resources of the MGM British studios and some of Shepperton's as well, his 90 tons of specially dyed sand, and his 36-foot high centrifuge, Kubrick transfers *Destination Moon* to the space age and wins the ultimate technical triumph in that his film is beautiful to watch from start to finish.

If there was any doubt that space travel will be the most spectacular adventure of mankind's future, *2001: A Space Odyssey* is the definitive affirmation that every last coin spent on the space race will be worth it. Kubrick's camera dances in an unrestrained love affair with the planets and with the curious, knobby craft that will forage between them, floating exuberantly through the light-years to the 'Blue Danube' waltz. His interiors are equally breathtaking, from the sheer white of the space-station dotted with stark red furniture to the huge circular room where the Jupiter-bound astronauts keep in trim by running round the ceiling or watch themselves being interviewed on flat television screens set into the lunch-table beside their dishes of food-paste. Best of all, there is a sense of fun that never obtrudes – the helmeted stewardesses who calmly turn upside down, the zero-gravity toilet with its immense list of essential instructions, the astronaut who is more concerned about his salary increase than about the significance of his voyage, and that splendid invention HAL-9000, the talking computer who admits, with a complacent flicker of equations, that it enjoys working with people.

It could so easily have been invalidated by some conventional narrative, a touch of spacesuit melodrama, a tidy ending. But *2001* takes the best from Arthur Clarke's original short-story, *The Sentinel*, and makes no attempt to overload it; Kubrick balances Clarke by demonstrating (as he did in *Dr Strangelove*) the extent to which mankind blunders from one missed opportunity to the next. Given the brainwave of using a bone as a

Contrasts in landscape: (right) Charlton Heston meets Kim Hunter for the first time on the *Planet of the Apes* (20th Century Fox, 1967). (right below) The lunar surface in *2001: A Space Odyssey* (MGM, 1968) where the black monolith waits to send out its warning to the universe.

weapon for food, the apeman's first act is to club one of his own kind with it. Given the facility of space-travel and the awesome splendour of the solar system, the 21st-century man dozes, gossips, makes banal remarks about sandwiches and takes snapshots. Given the technology to create a superhuman computer that does all but scratch the astronaut's back while controlling his entire spaceship, the human discovers that he has to dismantle the thing to survive at all. And finally a blazing display of alien concepts reduces man to an inarticulate embryo, the Starchild who, as Clarke admitted, isn't too sure what to do next. Like the apemen, he's ready to be pushed one more rung up the ladder – and then, maybe, he'll think of something.

Yet *2001* transcends its ironies, celebrating the sheer audacity of the human race. That men are capable of their own miracles is summarized particularly stunningly by the shot of the ball-like spaceship sinking majestically into its landing bay in the surface of the Moon, while tiny figures supervise calmly from a hive of observation points. A signal from another planet finds a group of men quickly ready to respond, hibernation techniques and all. An astronaut adrift in space is tracked down and collected with hardly a second

thought. And a berserk, seemingly inviolable computer is demolished as a result of the quicksilver ingenuity of its intended victim. The opportunism of man is undeniable, even if so much of his effort is wasted on banalities, and *2001* demonstrates his resilience convincingly enough for one to interpret the final hint of rebirth with confidence – and pride. If human ingenuity can create *2001: A Space Odyssey*, if it can place men on the Moon and bring them home again, it will surely send us someday to Jupiter and beyond.

Perhaps there'll be some people out there. And maybe they'd be willing to answer a few questions.

FAR OUT

Every passing hour brings the Solar System forty-three thousand miles closer to Globular Cluster M13 in Hercules – and still there are some misfits who insist that there is no such thing as progress – Ransom K. Fern.

The branch of science fiction known as 'sword and sorcery' satisfies all those who mourn the passing of dragons and unicorns, and swear by Edgar Rice Burroughs. For them, the galaxy is an adventure playground where favourite legends may be re-enacted in technicolour actuality, where Conan and John Carter, Elric and Doc Savage may even now be racing across the sands to rescue a chaste princess or foil a master-plan that would scatter the stars with living skeletons. Far outside the frontiers of our own trivial solar system there's enough space for all wishes to be fulfilled, every alternative to be gratified, each dream to come true. And given the speed of thought, we have no need to be restricted by the speed of light.

In the cinema it all begins with Buck Rogers, invented in 1929 and circulated by a rival to the Hearst group of newspapers; his exploits in the 25th century were so popular that Hearst needed to find a competitive hero of their own, and in 1934 he duly appeared in the form of Flash Gordon, drawn by Alex Raymond. With his virginal girl-friend Dale Arden, Flash saved the Earth from the terror-planet Mongo, a missile under the control of arch-fiend Ming the Merciless; his clean-limbed heroism, impersonated by Larry 'Buster' Crabbe in hair turned specially blond for the purpose, was the ideal subject for Universal's new spate of serials.

The first film of *Flash Gordon* (1936) was the most expensive, costing $350,000 for 13 episodes – even though some of the sets and music were borrowed from other productions like *The Mummy* and *Bride of Frankenstein*, and others consisted of little more than curtains and drumbeats. The budget went mostly on special effects, done with miniatures: fizzing rockets, metallic cities, crustaceous monsters and the like. It was such a hit that Flash Gordon made a *Trip to Mars* in 1938, and Buster Crabbe was in sufficient demand to turn into *Buck Rogers* (1939) before changing back to his accustomed role in *Flash Gordon Conquers the Universe*

(1940). Meanwhile, other heroes from the comic-strips had burst from their pages; *Dick Tracy* (1937), *Captain Marvel* (1941), *Captain America* (1943), *Batman* (1943), and *Superman* (1948). As the *Batman* remake illustrated in 1966, and the ponderously pornographic *Flesh Gordon* in 1974, those vintage serials had a flavour of square-chinned simplicity, itself a parody, that seems almost impossible to recapture today.

With affection, however, they are frequently recalled, and the magic names retold like an incantation to restore the less complex days of childhood. One dedicated admirer has been the American film-maker Harry Hurwitz, whose *The Penny Arcade* (1966) was dedicated to the inventor of Superman and told of a struggling cartoonist and his Walter Mitty dreams of becoming the invincible hero of his own comic strip.

Hurwitz renewed his homage with *The Projectionist* (1970), in which Chuck McCann, an amiable shambles in charge of a projection-booth, pictures himself as Captain Flash, an ineffectual but persistent combatant for the favours of Ina Balin. Attempting to conform to legend, Captain Flash nips into a telephone booth to strip from his everyday tramp guise to become the cloaked hero; unfortunately the booth is one of the

Comic-strip heroes: (far left) Larry 'Buster' Crabbe explains a new weapon to Philson Ahn (in helmet) and Constance Moore in *Buck Rogers* (Universal, 1939). (left) Chuck McCann and Ina Balin celebrate those days of innocence in *The Projectionist* (Maglan, 1970).

Figures of myth and fantasy. (right) Todd Armstrong in *Jason and the Argonauts* (Morningside Productions, 1963), one of the classic adventure stories brought to life by Ray Harryhausen. (below) Jane Fonda and Anita Pallenberg in *Barbarella* (Paramount, 1967).

modern kind, cramped and made entirely of glass, and Flash ends up on the pavement, trousers around his ankles, as an irritable passer-by interrupts to make a phone-call.

One of the happiest comic-strip films came from Czechoslovakia and won first prize at the Trieste Film Festival in 1966. Called *Who Would Kill Jessie?*, it was directed by Vaclav Vorlicek and began as another of his films for children; as the script developed, however, Vorlicek realised that something more serious was shaping up. The result is comedy in full measure, but with teeth. Jessie is the bursting blonde heroine of a comic strip in which she is hunted headlong through a series of unlikely and often sadistic encounters by a berserk Superman figure and a villainous cowboy. The strip happens to fall into the hands of a wife-pecked professor at a time when his inventions have run into snags, and he becomes so fascinated by Jessie's ability to escape from trouble by sheer technical ingenuity that he even dreams about her. Unfortunately his wife, whose university career is more successful than his, has just invented a somniograph – a device for watching dreams and eradicating nightmares – which has a side-effect of which she is unaware in that it also turns the nightmares into reality. Disgusted to discover her husband dreaming about another woman, she uses the machine on him. And so the voluptuous Jessie and her two destructive hunters materialize in the professor's flat.

As the snapdragon wife (beautifully played by Dana Medricka) proudly displays her machine at work on a cow amid a hushed crowd of surgically draped medical experts – who applaud reverently when the machine converts the animal's fly-blown nightmare to a lyrical vision of peaceful luxury – a voice murmurs: 'But have we the right to change dreams?' And the indestructibility of dreams is what the film reveals itself to be about; running hilariously riot, the incarnate dream characters wreak a succession of shattering changes in the professor's world until they are brought under control – at which point, naturally, the professor finds himself nearing his original, wife-pecked predicament.

Man's imagination has to be free to roam or man himself progresses nowhere. The film is sometimes too slapstick for its own good, with at least a couple of jokes that don't come off, but mainly it is sheer delight, thanks as much to the photography of Jan Nemecek (cameraman for Milos Forman) as to the splendour of Olga

Schoberova, all legs and frontage, who personifies Jessie. It has all the devil-may-care insanity of the strip-cartoon, plus the irony of a Pohl and Kornbluth satire.

It's not exactly 'sword and sorcery', though. The closest film to the tradition is perhaps Michael Waddell's *Neverwhere* (1967), in which yet another commercial artist finds himself transformed by a naked princess into a sword-swinging strong man, grappling with mutants who disappear when vanquished. When her sceptre has been recovered, the princess returns him abruptly to the 'present' (and from animation to live-action), but forgets to destroy the plans that show him how to build the tele-gate into her dimension, so there's room for a sequel. A nicely designed spoof, the film illustrates the origins for this kind of adventure – they reside in myths like the Odyssey or *Jason and the Argonauts* (given enjoyable treatment by Harryhausen in 1963), or the outrageous flights of fantasy told by *Baron Münchhausen* (unmatchably filmed by Karel Zeman in 1961 with a remarkable technique combining live-action and art-work).

With *Barbarella* (1967), a worthy space-age successor was found to these heroic jaunts. Directed by Roger Vadim and co-written by Terry Southern, it was based on the erotic strip-cartoon by the French illustrator Jean-Claude Forest, whose heroine, an emancipated, space-ranging lady of the year 40,000, spends most of her time in a state of charming undress – which represents all the weaponry she needs for protection. Forest was artistic adviser for the film, although in the faultless form of Jane Fonda (managing indisputably to shake free at last from her close resemblance to Henry Fonda in a blonde wig) his heroine spent sadly too much time obscured by clothing, her free-fall strip behind the credits left unfulfilled by later developments. The film is a splashingly decadent example of Vadim at his most vulgar, and anyone who finds it less than enjoyable had probably best stick to *Destination Moon*; Barbarella wades for no very clear reason through a jungle of pop-art designs and see-through sets, strewn with black leather, chains and inflatables, and dominated by the awesome Anita Pallenberg as the Black Queen, all eye-patch and growl. The two girls balance each other, in parallel to much of Vadim's other work (Martinelli/Stroyberg in *Blood and Roses*, Moreau/Stroyberg in *Liaisons Dangereuses*, Girardot/Deneuve in *Vice and Virtue*), while between them is the romantic image of Pygar, the blind angel who, being love, has no memory.

Bristling with seductive disposable décor, *Barbarella* is beautifully photographed by Claude Renoir and is so crammed with inventive extremes that it inspires a certain amount of fatigue at the two-thirds mark when the juvenile business of an invisible wall (plus invisible key) is introduced. But it is chiefly engaging for its humour, as with Barbarella's enjoyment of the Excessive Machine that is supposed to destroy her by over-pleasuring (but blows its own fuses instead), or the scene with undercover agent David Hemmings grappling with gadgets that don't function and messages that don't get through, his hair standing on end after an explosive glove-to-glove session with Barbarella. Its cosmic costumes designed by Jacques Fonteray, *Barbarella*, like its source material, is a series of magnificent fragments held together with colour and flesh – not too many swords but plenty of sorcery.

Vadim's success has been allowed to overshadow that of Mario Bava, one of Italy's leading cameramen since 1943, who has been making (and photographing) his own feature films since 1959, occasionally following the fashion for pseudo-American pseudonyms such as John M. Old. At least two of his horror films – *Mask of the Demon* (1960) and *Black Sabbath* (1963) are classics of the genre, but he has also made thrillers, psycho-dramas and science fiction, and in 1967 he made the comic-strip *Danger: Diabolik* based on the *fumetti* by Angela and Luciana Giussani. It starred John Phillip Law (who was also the angel in *Barbarella*) as the lithe lawbreaker, stealing the country's entire gold reserves and blowing up its tax records so that he can be a national hero as well as rich. A cross between Batman and the athletic underground conspirators of Feuillade's silent-screen adventure films, Diabolik – the hero – makes good watching, nipping up walls with the help of hand-held suction pads and making love to Marisa Mell on a bed of banknotes. As usual, Bava directs with a mixture of shock-cuts and sinuous camera movements, and his ending, with Diabolik buried alive in gold, is a splendid irony.

Bava specializes in returns from the grave. His most outlandish variation on the theme is in *Planet of the Vampires* (1965), in which Barry Sullivan lands in his horseshoe spaceship on a distant planet and finds that his crew immediately start to kill each other. Peace is temporarily restored, three corpses are buried, and as the camera prowls through the mists toward their graves the tall steel sculptures that mark the burial ground topple slowly and the spacemen emerge in their poly-thene shrouds. They have been taken over by alien spirits on the search for a new home since their own sun has died. At the end of the film they find it – the planet Earth.

In the furthest reaches of space, the visiting Earthman seems bound to meet his match sooner or later. In *Wild Wild Planet* (1965), by Bava's prolific rival Antonio Margheriti (masquerading under the name of Anthony Dawson but not to be confused with Grace Kelly's victim in *Dial M for Murder*), the United Democracies' space station Gamma One finds its streets full of artificial deflatable women collecting victims for spare-part surgery back in Delphos; they miniaturize their specimens and take them home in handbags. Featuring the ubiquitous Tony Russell and Lisa Gastoni, the film is crammed with happy notions, such as four-armed hit men, envy of the Mafia, who can keep their hands in

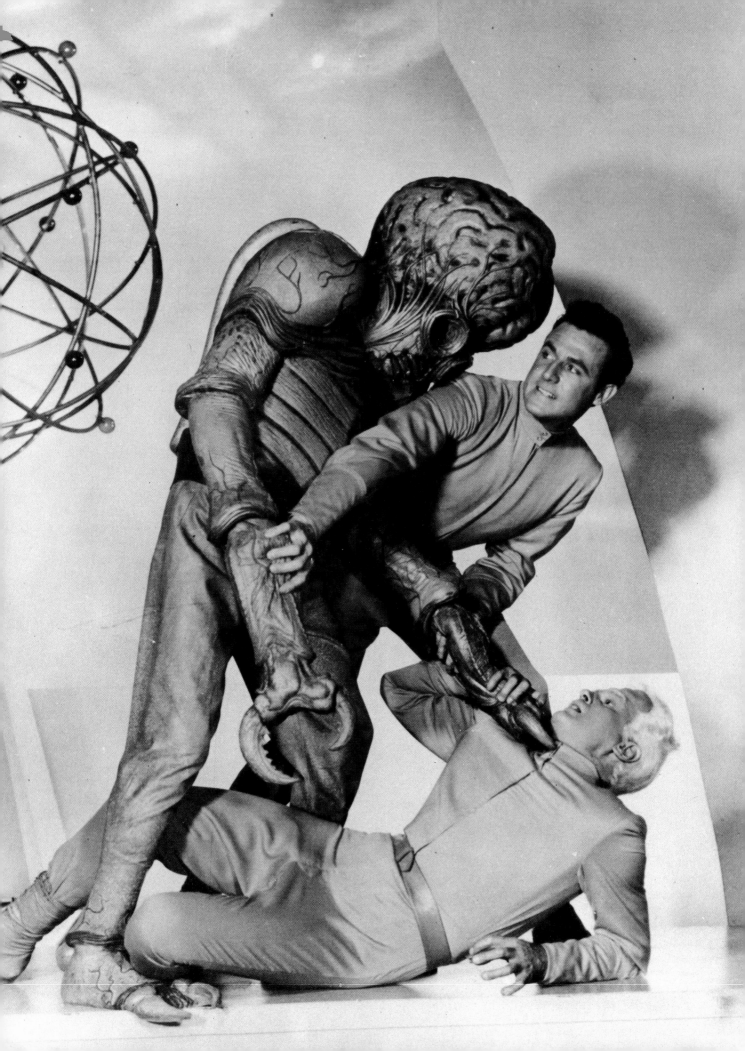

Intergalactic menace: Jeff Morrow, Rex Reason, and
Faith Domergue extract themselves from the Mutant's
clutches on the ruined world of Metaluna in *This Island
Earth* (Universal, 1955).

their pockets while strangling people. In *Phantom Planet*
(1961) it's miniaturization time again; Dean Fredericks
is reduced to a tiny nude inside his spacesuit on the
planet Rehton, whose inhabitants need help against the
Solarite menace. John Agar, trying to get away from it
all in *Journey to the Seventh Planet* (1961), gets as far as
Neptune in the year 2001 and meets, along with the
customary giant rats and spiders, a giant brain that gives
him hallucinations about the girls back home.

Russ Bender encountered the *Space Monster* in 1965;
it was accompanied by giant crabs and an alien resembling the recipient of a custard-pie gag. Roy
Thinnes had the most difficult problem of all, however,
in *Doppelganger* (1969); a planet is discovered on the
opposite side of the Sun, in the same orbit as Earth, and
when he gets there he finds he just left. The place is an
exact duplicate of home, but reversed like a mirror
image, and he has to retrace his journey to prove the
point, only to meet himself coming back. The *Thunder-
birds* models of Gerry Anderson and his team do little
to improve the situation, and the cast, including Herbert
Lom, Patrick Wymark and Ian Hendry, keep dis-
appearing in an alarming manner, perhaps in search of
an alternate universe.

Such trivia are put to shame by the two classics of the
1950s, *This Island Earth* (1955) and *Forbidden Planet*
(1956). The former was directed by Joseph Newman
from a novel by Raymond F. Jones, and after a slow
start it produces some of the best science-fiction images
the cinema has ever seen – the matter-transmitters that
transform their occupants to skeletons before beaming
them through space, the giant observation room on the

flying saucer, and the magnificent landscape of Metaluna itself, lurid with the destruction wrought by the
neighbouring world of Zahgon. Despite its lock-jaw
performances and ponderous dialogue, *This Island
Earth* gradually draws us into an extraordinary intergalactic adventure that eradicates the bland self-
confidence of the early sequences and justifies the film's
title only too clearly – our planet is an offshore fragment,
ignored by the politics of the universe, and there are
some advantages to be gained by this detachment. It's
a message in line with the 'things-we-aren't-meant-to-
know' theory, but it contains too the *War of the Worlds*
theme of evolutionary development, illustrated by the
high foreheads of the Metalunans (their leader nicely
played by Jeff Morrow), and the even higher forehead
of the clawed Mutant, past all reason and sanity, that
lurks in the corridors of a ruined planet.

In Fred McLeod Wilcox's *Forbidden Planet*, an invisible Caliban-figure lurks on Altair-4, set loose by the
brain of Dr Morbius after an overdose of Krell science.
This 'dark mysterious force' has destroyed all survivors
of the good ship Bellerophon except Morbius (Walter
Pidgeon) and his daughter (Anne Francis) who has
grown to a delectable young thing in miniskirts, given
to paraphrasing Shakespeare ('I always so terribly
wanted to meet a young man, and now here are three
of them at once. They're *beautiful!*'). The arrival of
Commander Adams (Leslie Nielsen) and his baseball-
team crew causes Morbius great concern, and he lends
them Robby the Robot, master of 187 languages, to
help prepare for departure once more. When the hint
doesn't work, Caliban prowls to the attack; caught in a
force-field, he slightly resembles the bulldog in Tom
and Jerry cartoons, but the 'electronic tonalities' which
accompany his onslaughts are wild and terrifying.

Quite apart from its immaculate appearance (mellow
Eastman colour and plenty of it on the Scope screen),
Forbidden Planet is fascinating in its delicate handling of
the incest theme. As the Morbius daughter, Alta,
naively responds to the attentions paid her by the crew-
men, the monster grows in size and fury; when she
settles for Adams and wants to go back to Earth with
him, Morbius is forced to face the truth – 'Even within
the loving father there exists the mindless primitive'.
In the climactic sequence, with Caliban burning a
way through impermeable metal 28 inches thick, the
symbolic penetration means his death as a father. 'My
evil self is at that door,' he screams, 'and I have no
power to stop it!' The tragedy is given added pathos by
the bright, artificial Eden of Altair-4, a haven for father
and daughter, serene with the wisdom contained in the
40-mile wide computer installed by the Krell, the
planet's former inhabitants, and which transcends the
petty laws of human competence. Too much knowledge
the film says, we know ourselves too well. 'About
a million years from now,' the Captain tells his crew
as Robby takes their saucer home, 'the human race will

have crawled as far as where the Krell stood.' We're not, after all, the gods we thought we were.

Although it settles for some conventional dunes and mountain ranges, albeit in unconventional colours, *Forbidden Planet* conveys the sense of an alien surface with memorable simplicity. Those same dunes and mountains seem to have been around ever since; a decent Earth-style jungle has seldom been discovered elsewhere. With *Fantastic Planet* (1973) the same sparse terrain is underfoot, but as the film is entirely animated there's room for some occasional bizarre growths, and they're fun when they happen – like the bunches of crystals that shatter at the sound of a whistle. Directed by René Laloux, *Fantastic Planet* is a French/Czechoslovakian co-production based on the novel by Stephan Wul, *Oms en série*, which is well-known in France but remains unknown among English-speaking science-fiction addicts. As adapted for the screen by Roland Topor, its story suggests that the reason Wul has not been widely translated is that his fantasy is rather ordinary stuff, its jumble of themes containing that of the sterile super-race, the tribal unit struggling to self-awareness, and the central character who manages to break from one society to the other. But *Fantastic Planet* does have its surprises, in particular with the revelation that the Draags (39-foot-tall androids with red eyes and blue skin) spend their mental energy controlling the choreography of Daliesque sculptures, headless statues on another world, and in general with the unexpected wild-life of the planet Ygam, populated with such as the monstrous caged being that laughs hysterically while swatting small pig-like flying creatures into the ground at random. It ends abruptly in utopian harmony, and appears to have suffered considerable pruning for Western audiences; what it really needed was a Morbius twist or two.

As an indication of just how simple science-fiction art can be, Piotr Kamler's *The Green Planet* (1965) was achieved apparently by sprinkling sand on a green background. Written by Jacques Sternberg, this delightful short describes the characteristics and customs of the zestful, star-shaped inhabitants of the planet Actur. For their chief industry, they make time – time to lose, time to gain, time to fill – and their favourite activity is disintegration and reincarnation. 'Although tone deaf, they love music,' announces the dead-pan commentary, 'and when one of them gets an idea he grows to enormous proportions.' Suddenly one realizes that the cheerfully absurd race being catalogued isn't alien at all, and the joke that while the Acturians are immortal their gods aren't, is then an effective body-blow.

Another example of French science fiction comes from Pierre Kast's *The Heat of a Thousand Suns* (1965), his first venture into animation, edited by Chris Marker (who made *La Jetée*). A young man in the far future becomes bored with the solar system he knows too

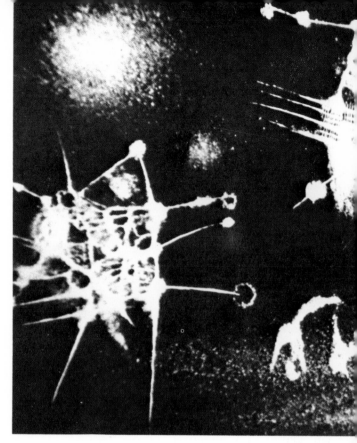

Animated science fiction. (above) The inhabitants of Actur, drawn with sand for *The Green Planet* (SOFAC, 1965). (below) Designs by Eduard Luis for Pierre Kast's *The Heat of a Thousand Suns* (Argos, 1965).

well and goes for an unrepeatable trip to the stars, in the company of his robots and his cat. On a remote planet he encounters a tranquil civilization where something has only to be wished for, and it happens; he meets a girl, they fall in love, and their romance is frustrated by his complete inability to recognize the different standards of her society where sexual groups of eight comprise a family. Put together from paintings by a Spanish surrealist artist, Eduardo Luis, whose suffused landscapes and delicate tapering figures provide the perfect balance to the gentle melancholy of the hero's monologue, the film has the same touch of scorn at its centre as was evident in Kast's other science-fiction works, *Amour de Poche* (1957) and *Les Soleils de l'Ile de Pâques* (1971), although its twinkling conclusion is more in keeping with his romantic comedy *Vacances Portuguaises* (1961). It's one of the most effective screen versions so far of science fiction's crusade not so much for a better world as for better people on it.

Animation has provided many disquieting images in science fiction, often in the form of parables from Eastern Europe, whose studios poured out cartoon warnings in the 1960s. In Poland, the dark talents of Jan Lenica and Walerian Borowczyk produced a number of classic fantasies, including *Labyrinth* (1963) and *Jeux des Anges* (1964), both of which portrayed hideous and repressive societies. In Lenica's *Labyrinth*, a bowler-hatted Icarus arrives at a city filled with mutant creatures – a dinosaur skeleton baying at the moon, humanoid reptiles hiding behind shutters and windows, a frock-coated lizard on human legs pursuing a girl. After sight-seeing, the visitor tries to leave, but vultures set upon him and leave his bones picked clean, falling through the sky. Borowczyk's *Jeux des Anges* opens with another arrival, by train, at a community seething with the assertion of its own distorted identity; the film's title suggests delicacy and charm, but these angels amuse themselves with an almost intolerable savagery. To the accompaniment of droning organ music, an endless succession of executions takes place, with featureless shaven heads rolling noisily down to collect in enormous boxes. Truncated pipes, and sawn-off wings lie about the place, and as one wing lies in state on a white-sheeted plinth, a stream of blue blood flows with agonizing beauty from its severed joint. Finally the train carries us away again, from Heaven, Europe, or what you will. But the organ music refuses to be left behind.

With his feature-length animated film, *Théâtre de Monsieur et Madame Kabal* (1967), Borowczyk created another nightmarish world, based, he said cheerfully, on 'symbols provided by life'. Just as the rituals of *Jeux des Anges* are determined by an established and scrupulously respected code, so the Kabals pursue an almost conventional morality in their concrete cottage situated on a wilderness split with chasms. Their existence is extraordinary, yet its rules are recognizably mutated from those of our own society. When Madame falls ill, the unfathomable wisdom of the medical profession operates on her with hooks, saws and grappling irons lowered from the sky. What matter that beneath a shower of truncated pipes, Madame scrubs her back with a thing like a boat-hook? Or that to satisfy her recovered appetite she consumes a kind of flying ant-eater, complete with the arrow that shot it down? These are casually commonplace events, small pleasures, small crises in the placid pattern of domesticity. Like any parable in which distortion leads to a closer 'reality', Borowczyk's films call into question the validity of our way of life by comparison with the one he shows.

Not far removed from *Labyrinth* is Gerald Frydman's *Scarabus* (1971), a first film of remarkable assurance which uses bowler-hatted, identical figures reminiscent of the nonentities in Magritte's paintings to populate a city of bleak façades interrupted by giant boulders. Literally tearing each other apart, although with casual curiosity rather than malice, the men struggle to see what lies behind a fence surrounding what appears to be a building site in the city centre. One of them makes it at last, and promptly falls into space through the hole in what is revealed to be a spinning coin. The camera pulls back, as it were, to show that the coin is one of many being spun by scores of little men in the streets of a city, and then pulls back even further to show that the city is the merest dot on the surface of an 'egg in a frying pan.

This method of putting us all in our place is a familiar enough theme in science fiction, where the similarity between the nucleus of an atom and the planet of a sun at the other end of the universe has been uneasily remarked upon more than once. On film, it was illustrated with dramatic simplicity by *Cosmic Zoom* (1968), a Canadian Film Board documentary which started from a gnat on a boy's hand and moved steadily outwards until not only the gnat and the boy but also the planet and the solar system are lost to view in the inconceivably vast numbers of galaxies in space. The camera then 'returns', rediscovers the gnat, and with a magnification finally reaching ten million million demonstrates that matter too is made up of countless specks in limitless space. Once man starts travelling out, or for that matter travelling in (like Matheson's Shrinking Man), his journey will be unending.

Whether such journeys will ever be made, and the effect they might have on the human condition, has always fascinated science-fiction writers, who tend to use the hermetic world of the long-distance spaceship to present hot-house miniaturizations of some likely futures of planet Earth. In *Outward Bound* (1930) and *Between Two Worlds* (1944), both based on the Sutton Vane play *Outward Bound*, the spaceship is full of elegant types who gradually become aware that they are all suicides on their way to face the divine judgment. The first batch included Leslie Howard and Douglas

Fairbanks Jr, the second John Garfield, Paul Henreid and Sidney Greenstreet. No destination is specified for the occupants of *Spaceflight IC-1* (1965), exploring space with colonization in view, but they'll be lucky if they get there; authoritarianism, friction and mutiny among an undistinguished cast indicate that another couple of generations should find them in the 'mindless savage' category, fighting and feuding among the stainless steel corridors.

The central figure of *Silent Running* (1971) is similarly unhinged, which has the unfortunate effect of invalidating his mission – that of protecting the only surviving botanical specimens of our poisoned planet. Since he appears so questionable a choice for the job, the subject of the film also appears unlikely, for instead of preserving its flora conveniently and economically to hand in greenhouses, Earth has packed them off into space in the care of fidgety recruits all too anxious to get back home again. The exception is played by Bruce Dern; where the others greet with joy the instructions from Earth to forget the whole thing, blow up the domed spacecraft and come on home, he is inclined to argue. He is even prepared to sacrifice the lives of his companions in order to protect the rather wilting foliage that has been under their care; this is the action he eventually takes, after which he steers off through the rings of Saturn and some brief psychedelics in an unformulated attempt to avoid being noticed by the authorities. During his long flight (and long it certainly is) he entertains himself with the help of little robots resembling mobile cocktail cabinets, which shamble about doing minor tasks in a jerky and uncoordinated manner seemingly guaranteed to bring about blown fuses in no time at all. They saw up a gash in his leg, attempt to master the subtleties of card-playing, and shuffle with embarrassment or tug shyly at sleeves in moments of affection. It's with their help that the final dome goes sailing off into the stars at the end of the film bearing all that's left of the green hills of Earth. Where Man has Failed, maybe the Machine will Succeed.

Directed by Douglas Trumbull, one of Kubrick's special-effects men for *2001*, the settings of *Silent Running* are clearly intended as its main attraction – in fact the trip through Saturn's rings was a concept considered but abandoned by Kubrick for *2001*. They have been lovingly planned and accomplished, from the slit-scan effect used to produce the 'trip', to the 26-foot model of the spaceship, incorporating 650 German army tank model kits. Cutting corners, the film cost $1,300,000, which makes it seem perversity to complain that it's actually *not* as glossy as the multi-million dollar *2001*, nor even as dramatic in appearance as many a lesser film. Were it not for the robots, *Silent Running* would be as boring as it is unconvincing – which makes it all the more astonishing that a group of students at the University of Southern California should have achieved *Dark Star* (1973) for around

$6,000 and created an odyssey that is, by comparison, both hilarious and inventively original.

The 'Dark Star' of the title is a spacecraft containing four men on an interminable mission to find and destroy any planets anywhere that are likely to cause a supernova by developing unstable orbits. The quest has rendered the crew and their equipment equally unstable; the bombs that they carry for demolishing planets have a certain level of intelligence and one of them keeps threatening to end it all by exploding prematurely, while what's left of the living quarters (after a meteor shower) is cluttered by an unpleasant and globular alien, adopted by one of the crew who now regrets his soft-heartedness and keeps trying to hunt it down. There is also of course a talking computer with a seductive voice (reminiscent of Barbarella's), which is supposed to keep everything functioning normally but is rapidly falling apart, while the former captain, dead but preserved in cold-storage, insists on discussing baseball through the electrodes planted in his brain. This chaotic situation reaches its climax when the talking bomb, stuck in the malfunctioning launching-bay, decides that it will explode regardless of the inconvenience this will cause; desperately the crew members try to talk it out of the decision, although by this time their own preoccupations have made it difficult for them to concentrate on anything practical – one of them is lost in dreams of his destiny among the stars, another imagines himself back in the surf at Malibu, while perhaps the sanest (played by Dan O'Bannon, who co-wrote the film and designed the special effects) has the uneasy suspicion that he's an impostor and shouldn't be on the ship at all. The conclusion is both macabre and funny, somewhat in the manner of *Dr Strangelove*.

One would have expected that satire of this kind could only come from the disenchanted West, but there are coincidental resemblances between *Dark Star* and the crumbling defeatism of the space-station in Andrei Tarkovsky's *Solaris* (1972), the most intelligent and questioning science-fiction movie ever made. Both films owe allegiances to the Czechoslovakian deep-space epic made ten years earlier, *Ikaria XB1* (eventually released in Britain in ruinously abbreviated form as *Voyage to the End of the Universe*). Amid Jan Zazvorka's brilliant and elaborate interiors, which were used and reused for several subsequent films, the first expedition to leave Earth on the hunt for life outside the solar system sets out to explore the planets of the star Alpha Centaurus, encountering on the way a 20th-century hulk still equipped with nuclear weapons and guarded by an eery crew of skeletons.

Continuing its journey, the Ikaria enters the sphere of influence of a Dark Star, which first sends one of the pilots berserk and then puts everyone to sleep. They are rescued by the sudden intervention of a protective screen beamed at them, they realize, by the life-forces

(above) Bruce Dern, the last ecologist, teaches his robot companions to play cards during their journey through the solar system in *Silent Running* (Universal, 1971).
(left) One of Jan Zazvorka's spacesuits in *Ikaria XBI* (Ceskoslovensky Filmexport, 1964).

they are seeking, and as they watch on the giant television screen in the control room the splendid spectacle of the architecture of a new planet is revealed to them. They hold up a new-born baby to watch, in anticipation of the Starchild. Directed by Jindrich Polák and co-written by Pavel Jurácek, *Ikaria XB1* is particularly fascinating for the craggy faces of the space-crew, resembling the illustrations of Kelly Freas brought to life, and for the meditative study of their everyday existence and its almost desperate emphasis on physical fitness and unflagging entertainment.

Athletics will form a vital part of mankind's future as the inevitable result of an increasingly leisurely existence, but where films like *Ikaria XB1* lay considerable stress on physical fitness for all, the films of the West hardly refer to the subject – or see it in the gladiatorial terms of *Tenth Victim* or *Rollerball*. A

strewn with rubbish, while one of the crew is dead and the other two hide in their rooms from experiences they refuse to discuss. Kelvin soon discovers the problem; after a night's sleep, he wakes to find his wife beside him, a beautiful girl called Hari, smiling in welcome as though they had never been parted. Ten years previously, back on Earth, Hari had committed suicide.

It appears that the planet Solaris, its surface an ocean of viscous, flowing patterns, is able to detect the fears and memories buried in the minds of its human observers and externalize these into living reconstruc-

The architecture of the future. (left) Two scenes from *The Andromeda Nebula* (Sovexportfilm, 1968).
(right) Unexplained constructions (above) on the surface of the planet Ygam, home of the Draags, in *Fantastic Planet* (Armorial, 1973). (below right) The visitors to Altair 4 wait by the protection of their flying saucer for the invisible Caliban to attack, in *Forbidden Planet* (MGM, 1956).

spectacular Soviet production, *The Andromeda Nebula* (1968), hearty with optimism about the epoch of complete harmony that awaits us in two thousand years, appeared to draw its cast entirely from the Olympic weight-lifting team, conducting their conversations while performing back-flips, diving into baroque swimming-pools, and absent-mindedly flexing their biceps. Despite some richly coloured special effects on an alien landscape, the film (which was directed by Eugene Sherstobytov from a Yefremov novel) leaves little other impression than that of rude health and an identical group of characters declaiming like opera stars.

It's certainly a long way from *Solaris*, in which everyone gives the impression of imminent collapse, and suicide has already overtaken a couple of the characters while the remainder grow haggard wondering whether to follow their example. The setting is a space-station hovering above the mystery planet Solaris, studied for many years by scientists unable to agree about its exact nature; solaristics now having become an unfashionable pursuit, the station is occupied by only three remaining specialists, whose reports have become so unintelligible that a 'space psychologist', Kelvin, is sent from Earth to investigate. He finds the place in a mess, untended and

tions, either several metres high on its own surface (as is described early in the film after a member of the research team has been lost), or life-size within the space-station. Each of the crew has his own 'visitor', a tangible hallucination too personal to be revealed – although we glimpse a nymphet blonde and a scuttling, dwarfish abomination. Kelvin's own worst recollection is his guilt at being the cause of Hari's death, and when Solaris resurrects this guilt in flesh and blood his first impulse is of course to reject it. He fires the girl off into space, but after his next sleep she has returned, or rather, a fresh copy of her has been provided. And since it's the psychologist's task to make his patients face the unfaceable, Kelvin has to come to terms with the living creature who insists on belonging to him. Hari is in fact so much a part of him that in the early stages of their relationship she cannot leave his presence without beginning to lose her shape; in one horrifying scene she tears her way through a steel door to rejoin him, falling in bloody tatters at his feet, her wounds healing instantly as he watches in amazement.

Later, she achieves independence, gradually becoming aware that she is something more than the original Hari, but at the same time that she is merely an extension of the Solaris ocean, existing only so long as she is on

(right) Kelvin (Donatas Banionis) hears from a former colleague Gibaryan (Sos Sarkissian) some warnings about the planet *Solaris* (Mosfilm, 1972). (left) Avalow (Sally Anne Newton) holds the container of all knowledge in John Boorman's *Zardoz* (Fox, 1974). (below left) Milo O'Shea prepares to submit Jane Fonda to the ultimate pleasure device in *Barbarella* (Paramount, 1967).

the space-station. While her affair with Kelvin duplicates the uneasy relationships of ten years before, Hari is also an observer for Solaris, capable of evaluating the difference between men's conscious and unconscious desires. When Kelvin's colleagues, somehow retaining a measure of sanity, work out a means of beaming his *conscious* thoughts at Solaris, the planet realizes its mistake and the 'visitors' cease to appear. The rational has been accepted, the irrational dismissed. But for Kelvin, past the point of rational thinking, another solution is necessary – and the planet, with infinite comprehension and sympathy, provides it.

Kelvin's country home, shared with his father, provides the unexpected Dovzhenko-style opening and even more startling close to *Solaris*, and there are several references back to this environment (becoming significantly more glacial) in which he is also seen as a child in the home-movie Kelvin shows to the new Hari. Where Stanislaw Lem's original novel signposted this territory but left it unexplored, preferring to expand upon the magnificent (but probably unfilmable) landscapes of Solaris's surface, Tarkovsky's film touches with a gentle nostalgia the elusive recollections of Kelvin's upbringing, the conflicting personalities of his parents and the bitter snowscapes of his childhood. Driven to recall the melancholy affection of his mother, Kelvin at last realizes why his marriage never had a chance, and where Lem ended in Quixotic ambivalence between hope and failure with a 'faith that the time of cruel

miracles was not past', Tarkovsky demonstrates – with something of a conjurer's flourish – that the miraculous is actively in evidence. Kelvin is transported to the next stage of his private self-analysis by being placed at the feet of a surrogate father.

Some interpretations of the film suggest that Kelvin was already on Solaris at the beginning, that birth and rebirth will follow each other for him in endless succession as the planet pursues its own god-like dreams, varying the story in minor details with each manifestation. The theory is appealing but a more linear interpretation seems ultimately more satisfying, to incorporate the clues provided by the Breughel paintings and the dripping water – aspects of Earth 'life' observed by Hari (on behalf of Solaris) during the film and consequently present in the planet's final reconstruction of Kelvin's environment. The power of *Solaris* is precisely that so many interpretations are available in its calm, hypnotic images; as a whole, it's the nearest the cinema has come to capturing the complexities of modern science fiction, with its intermingling of time and memory, its undertow of uneasiness, its emphasis on elegance and style. The immaculately photographed space-station, jumbled with incongruities surrounding a mellow library of useless conjecture, makes a superbly designed labyrinth of inarticulate loneliness, a memorable symbol of the disordered human mind. It seems unlikely that the furthest reaches of the universe could provide a more potent image.

Delphine Seyrig and Giorgio Albertazzi in Alain Resnais' *Last Year in Marienbad* (Cocinor, 1961).

Films, like people, are made of memories. The past is the ever-present on the cinema screen, a parade that keeps going by for as many times as one cares to reel it back to the starting post. To sit in the cinema is to recall, for image after image, an experience, an atmosphere, a set of emotions as vivid as they always were. And more than any other art form, the cinema has the power to make other people's pasts, and even more distantly other people's *versions* of their pasts (for as every historian is aware, the past is easily amended and improved), all a part of one's own. The point is well illustrated by Kurosawa's *Rashomon*, in which several witnesses give their account of the circumstances surrounding a murder; in a sense, it's irrational to prefer any one of the *Rashomon* yarns above the others – they each exist, and with equal force and equal truth,

TWISTERS

I have been here before
  But when or how I cannot tell;
I know the grass beyond the door,
    The sweet keen smell,
The sighing sound, the lights around the shore
                                    D. G. Rossetti.

for they are all *seen* to happen. Yet they are all fantasies, programmed and fed back through the different identities of the film's characters. The 'reality' never happened anyway, if one wants to be pedantic; but if one accepts that it did, if one is prepared to share the film's dream, from which 'reality' does one disengage? And how does one prevent the memory from retaining all the alternatives at the same time?

This multiplicity of recollection, in which the definition is crystal-sharp and the definitive an impossibility, has increasingly become a conscious theme in contemporary cinema, a vital factor in films as far apart as *Don't Look Now*, *A Bigger Splash* and *Monty Python and the Holy Grail*, but it is at its most vivid in the works of Fellini, Bergman, Resnais and Buñuel. Their films step calmly from the real to the non-real to the surreal, as convincing as any other image the memory is capable of creating, and they demonstrate, as science fiction has always insisted, that we live in a mirror-maze of alternate universes, switching from one to another according to the requirements of mind or body. If man is evolving, it is towards the ability to cope with stimuli operating with increasing complexity on several simultaneous levels. In such a context, the single-strand linear narrative can no longer be realistic – it will seem merely banal to a generation accustomed to absorb information from several inputs at the same time – and one might foresee that the science-fiction movie, reflecting this, will become indistinguishable from the popular 'mainstream' films that in turn will evolve from the experimental and underground cinemas of the 1970s and 1980s.

Films record the passage of time in a unique manner – they are physical proof that time can run backwards as well as forwards, existing simultaneously at an infinite number of points in between. They also *distort* time, stretching it (as in *Incident at Owl Creek*) so that one 'real' minute lasts thirty on the screen, or sweeping whole years aside with a fade-out or dissolve. Again this fluency matches that of the human memory – and of the imagination, which pays no attention to the ticking of clocks but will cheerfully fill a lifetime with durable summer afternoons. It should come as no surprise, then, although one greets the fact with startled recognition, that after writing *The Chronic Argonauts* in 1888, H. G. Wells linked his concept with that of the cinema so closely as to patent an audiovisual 'Time Machine' in 1895 which was to duplicate the experience described in his novel. Planned in collaboration with the British film pioneer Robert Paul, it was to be the original 'sensurround', with sliding walls, screens on all sides, and even wind machines to emphasize the sense of movement. Ironically, it was a project requiring more than money – it needed time, for the primitive projection equipment of the period to be developed to give a convincing illusion of past and future.

The Wells patent was never taken up, yet in a sense the Time Machine has been in operation ever since. As with *War of the Worlds*, the novel explored the implications of Darwinism, filtered through Wells's Victorian view of the ultimate structure of society – the obscene workers below, the feeble-minded idlers above – but what conveys the most potent image is not that of Weena and her flowers, nor of the bogeymen Morlocks, but the ruined library and, centuries later, the desolate beach in perpetual twilight, images which have returned repeatedly for science-fiction writers to contemplate in gloomy relish. And in the cinema, the perspectives of time-travel have constantly deepened and expanded since Méliès broke all 'natural' laws and made new sense of discontinuity.

As a gadget, the Time Machine itself has a memorable attraction, being a cross between an armchair and a bicycle, with intriguing knobs and dials and sections made of bronze, ivory and crystal. It was one of the few things the film of *The Time Machine* did full justice to when George Pal brought it to the screen in 1960, with Rod Taylor as the Traveller, Yvette Mimieux as Weena, and a number of bandy-legged extras with white hair and monster-masks as the Morlocks. The time-travel effects by Gene Warren and Tim Barr won a special Oscar, although they relied on stop-motion techniques dating back fifty years, but the obvious opportunity offered by the visit to Earth's dying centuries was overlooked completely. Instead, the film invented an atomic war in the immediate future, with the Traveller's home-town unaccountably swamped by a torrent of red lava. And while one might argue that this is in keeping with Wells's gloomy outlook, the film makes nonsense of his main theme by turning the Traveller into a rabble-rousing leader who stirs the Eloi to revolt against their fate at the hairy hands of the Morlocks, for all the world like a red-neck reincarnation of the sheriff in *High Noon*. Contrary to Wells, Pal evidently felt it was possible to turn the clock back . . .

Since one's cinema seat was the simplest and most accessible kind of time machine, as Wells had anticipated most of the stories told on the screen were in a sense time-travel stories; where journeys in time occurred as part of the plot, they were effected by vaguely magical means, and for romantic reasons. With the apparent exception of an obscure one-reeler made by Ashley Miller and J. A. Norling in the United States, *The Sky Splitter* (1922), in which a bomb-shaped rocketship with aeroplane-style wings flew faster than light and enabled its occupant to see the events of his own childhood, the earliest mechanical aid to time-travel offered by the cinema seems to have been a 'Time Ball' in Walter Forde's *Time Flies* (1944), a Tommy Handley comedy in which he and his team were sent back to the time of Shakespeare. Otherwise the fourth dimension was the province of speculative philosophers like Dunne and Ouspensky, from whose theories of Serial and Circular Time were derived a number of J. B. Priestley's plays in the 1930s with their hallmark of insecure fatalism

– time, like ghosts and the weather, followed its own inscrutable and unpredictable logic, and mortals could only observe and wonder or learn the error of their ways (as in *An Inspector Calls*, finally filmed in 1954).

It was magic that sent Leslie Howard back 150 years in *Berkeley Square* (1933), there to meet Heather Angel and add a new complication to the course of true love. The story was repeated with the equally vulnerable Tyrone Power in *I'll Never Forget You* (1951), but variations on the theme of the irresistibly charming ghost are to be found in, for example, *Forever* (1921) which was remade as the more famous *Peter Ibbetson* with Gary Cooper in 1935, Cocteau's *L'Eternel Retour* (1943), which combined Ouspensky with the Tristan and Isolde legend, and William Dieterle's *Portrait of Jennie* (1948), in which Jennifer Jones haunts Joseph Cotten until he has finished her portrait and can join her in the spirit world.

In the 1950s, time-travel continued to be a rather hesitant business on the screen, although science-fiction writers like Heinlein, Bester and Ward Moore were treating it with cheerful fluency. Henry Kuttner's *The Twonky* was an aggressive home appliance resembling a radio, built by a technician who through a 'temporal slip' found himself in the wrong factory; in the story, it peevishly disintegrates its luckless owners, but in Arch Oboler's film (1953) it becomes a television set with a

A group of welcoming hostesses in one of the chapters of *The Saragossa Manuscript* (Kamera, 1964).

hypnotic ray and is eventually vanquished by Hans Conreid – a story more in line with the 'how-to-cope-with-aliens' syndrome of the period. Charles Eric Maine wrote one of the classic fourth-dimension stories with *Timeliner*, but it was his lesser story *Timeslip* (1955) – also known as *The Atomic Man*, and finally published as *The Isotope Man* – that was filmed by Ken Hughes, with Gene Nelson and Faith Domergue. It featured the idea that an accident during an atomic research programme would put a man's mind seven seconds ahead, but did nothing with it other than indulge in fairly conventional detective-yarn melodrama. The most original piece of writing for the screen on this subject came from Charles Griffith and Mark Hanna, who constructed for Roger Corman the remarkable fantasy *The Undead* (1956), in which a prostitute is discovered to be the reincarnation of a girl executed as a witch in medieval times. Sent back to rescue herself, she realizes that her intervention will destroy a whole succession of futures, and she lets the execution go ahead. Rich with incongruities and anachronisms, the film is a charade but a potent one, made with relish, humour and a blinding efficiency;

with its intermingling of present and past and its emphasis on a two-way responsibility, it makes a fascinating precursor to the Corman films of the Poe stories.

After George Pal's *Time Machine*, general interest in the theme seems to have revived, beginning with *The Time Travellers* (1964), in which a girl 107 years in the future is called Reena as a nod to Wells's heroine. Written and directed by Ib Melchior, the film made up for the cinema's earlier neglect of the subject by throwing in a wide variety of accessories, including mutants, deviants, androids and the 'closed-time' theme, which traps the travellers in an ever-repeating circle of events at the end. The story was a re-run of the idea that the future will be an endless struggle between mutant surface-dwellers and underground scientists, but it is inventively told, with tolerable performances, lively special effects by co-writer David Hewitt, and – as a special bonus – a guest appearance by Forrest J. Ackerman. Also in 1964 the screen's closest approach to Ward Moore's alternate-USA novel, *Bring the Jubilee*, was seen in the form of Herschell Lewis's bloodbath *Two Thousand Maniacs!*, in which a Southern town avenges itself for having been wiped out during the Civil War by reappearing from time to time to capture and torture tourists from the North. Another off-beat, almost unclassifiable venture into the hypothetical was Wojciech Has's *Saragossa Manuscript* (1964), an immense, rambling version of Jan Potocki's eccentric 18th-century story-within-a-story incorporating rationalism, science, magic and most of the leading stars of Film Polski (Zbigniew Cybulski, Adam Pawlikowski, Elzbieta Czyzewska, etc). A cross between the Arabian Nights and *Last Year in Marienbad*, it flicked time and logic into fragments and chuckled to itself over the resulting confusion.

Before looking in more detail at the other films that took their cue from *Marienbad*, we should note the more conventional successors to *The Time Machine*. There was *Dimension 5* (1966), with Jeffrey Hunter and France Nuyen using their time-converter belts to nip three weeks into the future to uncover Chinese H-bomb shipments concealed in rice; and there was *Cyborg 2087* (1966), with Michael Rennie escaping from a future dominated by the radio-telepathy device inconsiderately invented by Eduard Franz in 1966 and persuading him not to invent it after all. Rennie, it seems, is half-human, half-machine, and he is pursued by two similar devices aiming to preserve the status quo; the inventor doesn't care for any of them much and he proves happy to render the future more habitable. With William Castle's *Project X* (1967) the Chinese are again on the attack, this time with fiendish medieval plagues in the year 2118; based on novels by L. P. Davies, it's a time-travel story with a difference in that information in the head of a 'processed' agent can only be unscrambled by making him believe he's back in the 1960s. With

Journey to the Centre of Time (1967), David Hewitt expanded his *Time Travellers* narrative to include a laser-beam war in 6968 AD and a battle with a pre-historic monster in 1,000,000 BC, concluding once more with the 'closed-time' idea and a threadbare budget. This time, Weena became Vina and was played by a lady credited as Poupee Gamin, about whom nothing further, unfortunately, is known.

Adapted from John Wyndham's short story *Random Quest*, Ralph Thomas's *Quest for Love* (1971) transferred physicist Tom Bell to an alternate universe where Everest is still unconquered, there's no Vietnam war, and John F. Kennedy remains alive. Having won the love of Joan Collins just as she dies of an incurable heart condition, the physicist returns to his 'real' time and searches for her equivalent. Nicely performed, the film suffers from an aimlessness of mood, starting with an air of bright comedy but wandering into deafeningly orchestrated and rather pointless romantic melodrama. Like the other 1971 time-dislocation adaptation, *Slaughterhouse Five*, it had all the awareness of being on to a good thing but lacked much idea of what to do with it.

Kurt Vonnegut's *Slaughterhouse Five*, not in fact his best novel but the first to go careering up the best-seller list, merges the two Vonnegut territories – factual and fantastic – into one extraordinary landscape. Billy Pilgrim, floating in bewilderment through his life as if it belonged to someone else, is present at the destruction of Dresden in 1945 and is simultaneously the occupant of a glass show-case on the planet Tralfamadore where he lives with the voluptuous actress Montana Wildhack and entertains the natives with performances of such traditional Earth rituals as eating, sleeping and sex. The two extremes are equally incredible: if one has to accept the fact of Dresden, one might as well accept the Tralfamadorians whose view of time is that whatever happens is always unalterably happening whether one is conscious of it or not. Billy Pilgrim, who has become 'unstuck' in time, bounces haphazardly around his life like a ball in a slot machine, triggering the lights and the sounds of memory (ours and Vonnegut's) and throwing a light at random across the unchanging surface of his existence. Through the juxtaposition of his 'normal' and his Tralfamadorian experiences, Billy's predicament illustrates the Vonnegut message that what we do is always with us, that there will always be a World War II, and that Dresden will always burn.

Not so much a science-fiction story, then, as an anti-war subject. It was no ordinary production either: *Slaughterhouse Five* had a budget of over three million dollars and was entrusted to George Roy Hill, fresh from the commercial success of *Butch Cassidy* (and destined to recover from his Vonnegut venture, which flopped, with the even greater success of *The Sting*). Hill's problems had less to do with reconstructing Dresden (he used Prague), or showing the surface of

Unstuck in time: (left) Roger Jacquet in Robert Enrico's
Incident at Owl Creek (Centaure/Filmartic, 1961). (below)
Montana Wildhack (Valerie Perrine) and Billy Pilgrim
(Michael Sacks) on the planet Tralfamadore in
Slaughterhouse Five (Universal, 1971).

Tralfamadore (he used wobbly special effects), than
with the visualisation of Vonnegut's humour – a stream
of sly, elusive jabs and abruptly hilarious incongruities.
He winds up with a war movie in which the central
character has wilder hallucinations than those endured
by the pacifist in *Catch-22*, but that's all. Whereas
Vonnegut makes all levels of Pilgrim's progress look
equally crazy, Hill makes the war scenes only as surrealistic as war itself, not more so. And whereas the
book gives no sign that the circle will be broken, the
film falls into the trap of a happy and escapist conclusion that would have delighted the Tralfamadorians,
with their scorn for the narrow vision of Earthmen.
Billy and Montana sit contentedly in their insulated
globe as though the nightmare, once past, is also past
renewing.

For the genuine film equivalent to Vonnegut, we
must look to films that are equally unconventional;
Billy Pilgrim is closer to the incredulous wanderers in
Orphée (1950) and *Le Testament d'Orphée* (1959) than
to the wisecracking myths of *Butch Cassidy*, not because
his origins go any further back than the pulp magazines
but because his existence encompasses thought, memory,
imagination and actuality with an equal emphasis. Like
Vonnegut, like Ouspensky. Cocteau dealt with circul-
arities, with deaths and resurrections occurring as part
of a grander scheme than man has any particular right
to understand. His farewell to the cinema, *Le Testament
d'Orphée*, stages and restages his own death, along with
a jumble of events, preoccupations and friends who
were important to his life, their presence viewed with
amiable serenity. To some extent his place in French
cinema has been taken by Alain Resnais, who made
with his short films in the 1950s and his first feature,
Hiroshima Mon Amour in 1959, the same case as *Slaughterhouse Five* for giving the past the same respect as the
future. If it is possible to derive from *Hiroshima* the
melancholy comfort that even the most atrocious events
can become forgotten, this interpretation of the film is
quickly contradicted by Resnais's later works, in which
both present and future are rendered insubstantial by
the uncertainties of the past.

Since it's possible to argue any number of meanings
into Resnais's *Last Year in Marienbad* (1961) it needs
little defence as a science-fiction movie, or for that
matter as a detective story, according to preference. It's
a deliberately 'open' film, in which past and present,
real and imaginary, are left unidentified and the central
question remains unanswered: did a married woman

(Delphine Seyrig) really meet last year in Marienbad
the stranger who now claims her while they are guests
at an immense baroque palace with a huge formal
garden? 'My aim', said Resnais, 'was to create a circling
interplay of feelings in the same way that in a modern
painting the interplay of forms succeeds in becoming
more important than the story.' And it was the haunting
mood of the film, the unnerving elegance of its gliding
camera movements through the palatial corridors, the
frozen gestures of its characters, that made it such a
powerful influence on the film-making styles that
followed. After *Marienbad*, a new kind of freedom came
to the cinema which is still being explored – sometimes
with unwatchable results – while the flash-shot which
could be memory or fantasy has already become a
cliché.

Resnais was not, of course, the only influence at
work: this was the time, for example, of Godard and
Truffaut and the new-found fame of Antonioni, whose
films also dwelt on the insubstantial and the spectacularly
ambiguous. In the same year as *Marienbad*, the French
director Robert Enrico made *Incident at Owl Creek*,
based so successfully on Ambrose Bierce's story from
the American Civil War that it looks as if it was filmed
at the time; it too dealt with the imagination – that of a
man about to be hanged, who appears to escape at the
last minute. It won the Golden Palm at Cannes in 1962,
the year in which Resnais's film editor, Chris Marker,
made *La Jetée*, one of the best-known science-fiction
short films, which again dealt with time-travel and
memory. Like *Owl Creek*, it's the story of a doomed
man drawn to the girl he loves regardless of physical
barriers; in the case of *La Jetée* he's a survivor of World
War III among a small group whose sole chance of
continued existence lies in making contact with the
future. Developing a method of time-travel by repeated
injections, they require the traveller to focus on the
strongest image in his memory – which happens to be
the face of a girl he saw at Orly Airport as a child.
Eventually he manages to make contact with her, to
remain physically in her presence for as long as he likes
until hauled bodily back into the 'present' where
Jacques Ledoux presides frowningly over the remnants
of mankind. Now a confirmed time-traveller, he is put
to the most difficult test of all – being sent into the far
future where a strange race awaits him, jewels like a
third eye in the centre of their foreheads. And when, his
mission accomplished, he finds his way back to Orly,
he is shot down by one of his co-survivors just as he
approaches the girl, while a child watches nearby.

Marker tells the story with stills, so effectively used
that one is seldom conscious of the lack of movement –
indeed the film 'moves' all the time, with dissolves and
panning shots. Quite apart from the superb brooding
quality of these photographs, with their shadowed
faces and sinister masks, they represent a re-phrasing of
time in themselves, frozen (like the creatures in the

museum visited by the time-traveller and the girl) in attitudes of unalterable existence. When Resnais made what was unarguably a science-fiction film in 1967, *Je t'aime, je t'aime*, it told very much the same story, although without the atomic warfare: again a man is injected with a memory-releasing fluid, and again he is drawn back to the girl who represents all that has been important in his life. Trapped between past and present, he flashes as if on elastic from one incident to another, until the events that led to his present situation have all been revealed: the girl had died, he blamed himself, and had attempted suicide. As he 'relives' the suicide, the shock breaks open the trap in which he has been caught, and the scientists supervising the experiment find his body lying on the lawn outside their laboratory.

It is tempting to interpret *Je t'aime, je t'aime* as the kind of yarn in which the key moments of a man's life are permitted to unreel before our eyes at the instant of death. Certainly there is room for the argument that the relationship between the time-traveller Claude and the girl around whom his travelling revolves, Catrine, is so beguiling in its own right that the science-fiction trappings are unnecessary – and one could go further and suggest that the plainly organic design of the time-sphere (a lumpy mixture of brain, heart and womb which contains him while the injections take effect) is a symbol for Claude's own body into which his soul has been thrust like a condemned man into a gas chamber.

The team of scientists, however, cheerfully packing their victim off into the past in the company of an equally powerless white mouse, provide the necessary context for the story; like the tribunal in *Orphée*, confronting the near-deceased with the events of his life, or like Frankenstein himself, restoring life and death to protoplasm that has already had enough of both, they take charge of Claude's existence as if they know better than he does what to do with it. The pathos of his predicament is that, like Ouspensky's Ivan Osokin, Claude is *aware* that this is his second time around and equally aware that he will continue to be unable to change its course – even that basically he doesn't *want* to change the events leading to his suicide attempt. And more than any other Resnais film, *Je t'aime, je t'aime* (the repetition in the title is appropriate to the recurrences in the story) is concerned less with personal reconciliation than with the struggle to define and come to terms with the processes of time, which robs one of experience even as one enjoys it. At one point, Claude even talks to T.I.M.E. on the telephone, its voice droning on without attention to his banal remarks, and the most striking of the film's many memorable images of attempted contact is of a drowning man in a telephone booth, an unexplained interjection that sums up the need to leave some kind of message before one's time runs out. With this beautiful, complex and much-neglected film, Resnais has much to tell us if he can only get through.

Made in the same year as the Resnais film, Ingmar

Bergman's *Hour of the Wolf* was another reconstruction of a man's life through an assembly of incidents from his past, the difference being that in this case (as with Bergman's *Persona*) the reality and the fantasy are so closely tangled that one can never be certain which is which – except at moments of disconcertingly obvious insanity as when a man floats up to the ceiling. The film's central character is an artist who has disappeared under mysterious circumstances from the island where he has lived for some years with his wife; as she recalls the events leading up to the disappearance it becomes clear that her husband felt himself ridiculed by their neighbours on the island and so persecuted by them that he is literally torn apart by their scorn at the end. The trouble with this story is that we only have the wife's evidence to go on, based in turn on her husband's diary which wanders hysterically through all kinds of nightmares that are recorded as if they were solid truth. Bergman is making a stingingly accurate point that artists can only work on the basis of what is inside themselves and the truths they uncover are as much personal as general. His films constantly emphasize the fact that they *are* films – artificial devices which attempt to express through images concepts normally too abstract to be defined.

Also in 1967, Roger Corman made his assault on inner space with *The Trip*, an attempt to show on film the kind of dislocations in time and memory caused by LSD. Peter Fonda downs a pill in the ornate hillside residence of a wealthy friend (a beautifully sympathetic performance by Bruce Dern in his pre-*Silent Running* days), and within twenty minutes is well on the way towards losing every possible link with the everyday world. People and events from his past and present surroundings become drawn into a succession of fantasies, erotic, nightmarish, bizarre – and often extremely spectacular – culminating in the total dis-

Assaults on inner space.
(left) Max von Sydow in
Bergman's *Hour of the
Wolf* (Svensk, 1967). (right)
Peter Fonda meets the
creatures from his night-
mares during *The Trip*
(AIP, 1967). (below)
Claude Rich is poised
beside the time-sphere in
Je t'aime, je t'aime (Fox,
1967).

integration both of 'reality' (shown through increasingly fast cutting) and of himself (the final shot is a
fragmented close-up). Reality in *The Trip* is an elegant
couple standing on the surface of a stretch of water (for
a television commercial), a wife who talks of lawyers
and divorce where neither are wanted, two nude girls
shuddering endlessly to beat music in a rock-club, a
curlered woman in a laundromat in the middle of the
night, a television broadcast on Vietnam and frenzied
neon signs. Unreality is two hooded horsemen on a
seashore, a burning sacrifice in a crypt, faces that spew
coloured lights, lovemaking, a tiny merry-go-round in
a tinsel interrogation room, an indefinable sense of fear.
'Isn't the real world good enough for you guys?' demands an angry waitress – and the ugly chaos around
her provides the immediate answer.

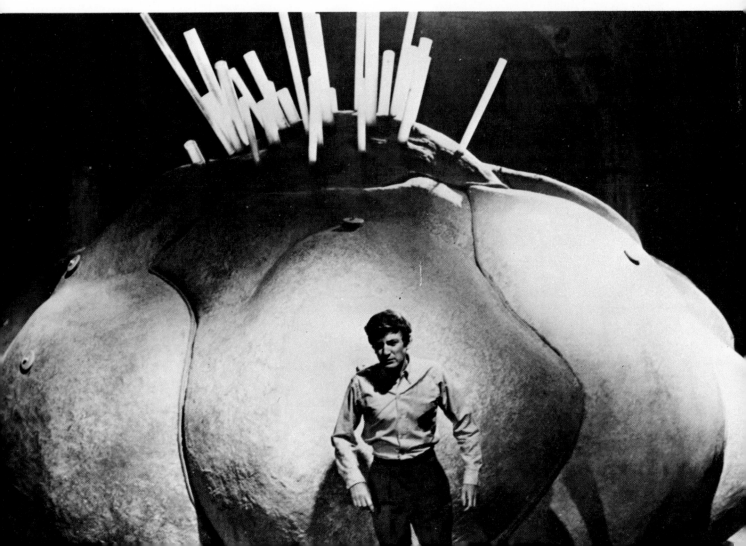

Images of dislocation. (left)
Laura Betti achieves the
miracle of levitation in
Pasolini's *Teorema* (Aetos,
1968). (right) Nightmare
visitors in Bunuel's
*Discreet Charm of the
Bourgeoisie* (Fox, 1972).

Culminating what turns out to have been a great year for 'new wave' science-fiction movies, 1967 also brought us Michael Snow's *Wavelength*, which consisted of a slow zoom from one end of a room to the other, taking forty minutes to complete the journey. Unbelievably, it's a great deal more than boring, although boredom is a necessary part of its psychology at about the fifteen-minute stage. It turns out to be funny, suspenseful, action-packed, absorbing and brutal, a biographical description of a finite period in what one recognizes as an infinite span of the room's existence. Bearing a high emotional charge that no team of script-writers could have bettered, *Wavelength* forces on you, if you stay the course, a valuable reassessment of what film can or should do. The *Marienbad* of the experimental cinema, it has seen scores of imitations, just as in its turn it was derived from the Warhol 'minimal cinema' technique; but in science-fiction terms its importance is that, like the novels of J. G. Ballard, it offers an insight into the extraordinary additional dimensions of the

apparently commonplace. A simple room, it seems, is crammed with alternate universes.

Whether or not the general audience is at all interested in alternate universes is debatable, but cinemagoers must undoubtedly have become accustomed to 'shorthand' film-making since 1967, that is, films in which time-jumps occur without explanation and in which images are presented without comment, leaving the audience to draw what conclusions they can. For too brief a period, this was the style of Pasolini, who with *Teorema* (1968) and *Porcile* (1969) created two brilliant and savage parables that flicked through a full spectrum of social activity – political, sexual, artistic and religious – and found nothing that can be trusted, nothing that endures. With images of an extraordinary crystal beauty, he shows cannibalism, bestiality, levitation, a whole catalogue of madness intercut with shots of bleak volcanic dust, his spokesmen tottering naked across a wilderness of demolished ideals. In Pasolini, the desert landscapes of the science-fiction films of the '50s have

understandably irritated and alarmed, and spends the rest of the film trying to sort out the truth with the aid of his speaking computer that makes predictions about everything from the weather to its owner's life expectancy. But at the end, the delicious Miss Karina is on horseback once again and the story is all set for an action replay.

The interchange of fact and fancy, if acceptable as a characteristic of the modern science-fiction movie, makes Luis Bunuel the greatest exponent of the genre in the history of the cinema, despite his assertion that 'my hatred of science and technology will perhaps bring me to the absurdity of a belief in God'. Although his purpose is vituperatively satirical, his method has increasingly been to discard all conventional time-structures in his films just as he has discarded the conventional in subject and behaviour in his stories. His work is famous for such vehement images as the sliced eye-ball in *Chien Andalou* and the pastiche of the Last Supper in *Viridiana*, through which he attacks the icons one had supposed to be inviolable and reveals (as Ballard's story about the Kennedy assassination reveals) that information and interpretation are matters of personal choice. A crucifix can contain a switchblade knife, a skipping rope can be used for hanging, a saint can from the highest motives spread catastrophe in his wake. Bunuel is concerned not with explanations but with ambiguities which, he says, 'reign high and low over all our acts and all our thoughts', and his images are intended to carry an intuitive charge – whether one consciously 'translates' them or not, they get through to the subconscious and set it vibrating like a gong.

In 1967, another breakthrough was *Belle de Jour*, in which Bunuel made the step from showing characters in the grip of fantasy to showing the fantasies themselves with an equal clarity and emphasis (although it was a small enough step to take from the hallucinations of *Simon of the Desert*). By the time of *Discreet Charm of the Bourgeoisie* (1972) and *The Phantom of Liberty* (1974) the deceptive clarity of the cinema image was being used by Bunuel to present a series of anecdotes in which the only certainty is the unexpected. *The Phantom of Liberty* is in fact full of familiar science-fiction situations based on the reversal of the everyday: obscene photographs are pictures of tourist landmarks, a sniper who has killed 18 people is declared guilty and released to public acclaim, a little girl who has 'disappeared' helps the police in their efforts to find her again, and defecation is performed sociably around a table while eating is shamefully pursued in private. Such eloquent irreverence, expressed with the stylish assurance of a master craftsman, marks the highest point that science fiction – and, it could be argued, *any* fiction – has achieved in the cinema.

But cult movies and cult directors are a long way from the uninhibited popular entertainment represented by the science-fiction films of the 1950s, and to pursue

been hauntingly updated.

The naked spokesman in *The Swimmer* (1968) is Burt Lancaster, playing one of the cinema's most pathetic time-travellers: a Connecticut health-fiend, he vows to 'swim home' across the pools in his neighbours' gardens, greeted with varying degrees of apathy by each, and as his journey proceeds we gradually learn that he is a self-made outcast, his wife and family long departed, his destination an empty house. Directed by Frank Perry, it's a simple but unsettling story, depending for its strength on the extent to which one wishes to interpret the symbols. The same could be said of Robert Benayoun's *Paris n'existe pas* (1969), in which a young painter begins to doubt the reality of his surroundings and finds by this means a route into the past where he falls in love with a girl whom, ghost-like, he cannot touch. Benayoun works in the surrealist tradition, using documentary footage to challenge his audience to identify the present, past and future, and proving that with film they are all one and the same. Another French director, André Farwagi, made a rather more melo-dramatic time-twister in the same year, *Le temps de mourir*, which begins with Anna Karina galloping out of nowhere on a white horse and crashing into a tree. She loses her memory but drops a spool of film that shows a murder being committed, and is then taken to the house of the man whose murder is recorded on the celluloid; as he has never been murdered in his life, he is the argument that, for example, *Fellini's 8½* or *El Topo* or *Un soir un train* are neglected masterpieces of the genre, is to stray into unnecessarily contentious territory. The science-fiction fan knows exactly what he's looking for in the cinema, based on his upbringing as a reader of *Astounding* or of *New Worlds*, and whether he likes *Marienbad* for being ahead of its time or loathes *2001* for being thirty years out of date, his verdict on their science-fiction qualities is less important than his opinion of them as films. Considered as a kind of crusade, the science-fiction cause is doubtless helped by the adoption of Luis Bunuel among the ranks of its converts, but to

The challenge of the head. Sean Connery rises from the harvest to disrupt the workings of the most dangerous computer ever developed. Scenes from Boorman's *Zardoz* (Fox, 1973).

label *The Phantom of Liberty* as first and foremost science fiction is more likely to act as an irritant than to persuade anyone it's a better film. The argument that Bunuel and Pasolini are in direct succession from George Pal and Jack Arnold may have a certain force, but it needs delicate, not militant handling.

More importantly, the science-fiction fan needs to be open to the special qualities of film as a means of expressing moods, fears and ideas – to accept a film like *Zardoz*, in fact, *not* for its originality in science-fiction terms but for its extraordinary achievement as pure cinema. Ironically, John Boorman's *Zardoz* (1973) was in the tradition of the 1950s by virtue of being a solid commercial success, although the science-fiction fans in general disliked it intensely. The story of the film is Boorman's own, but it has many honourable precedents, so many, indeed that although its time-twisting factor is perhaps its most significant element it could as appropriately be discussed under any of the chapter headings in this book. Set in the post-atomic age of 2293, it reveals a barren wasteland where marauding bands of near-savages, the Exterminators, wage tribal warfare under the guidance of a giant stone head that floats down periodically from the sky to cheer them on and supply weapons and ammunitions from between its teeth.

One of the Exterminators, Zed (Sean Connery), who is brighter than his fellow-tribesmen, dares to challenge the divine nature of the stone head by stowing away inside it. Pistol in hand, he is carried to the Vortex, a placid community where a super-computer guarantees immortality by preserving the memories and experiences of all the inhabitants; called the Eternals, they live in unending boredom and sterility, their crimes punished by interminable old age, their occasional suicides by prompt resurrection. Fascinated by Zed, they argue over his fate; one group, headed by Consuella (Charlotte Rampling) wants him destroyed, while another, headed by May (Sara Kestelman), insists that he should be studied for a while. During the contest that follows, Zed acquires an encyclopaedic knowledge of the Vortex and its purpose, confronts the forces that enclose it, and restores to its delighted, centuries-old inhabitants the ability to remain dead when they die. The process of evolution is released again and the natural history of man can resume its course.

The ashen wastes of the Outlands, where the Exterminators in their frowning Zardoz helmets ride in pursuit of the Brutals (shabbily suited like tired businessmen), have been the familiar setting for many a disaster novel. The Vortex, smugly enclosed within its force shield, is like many a glowing citadel awaiting a sword-and-sorcery Hero to broach its walls. And there have been many generations of space pioneers sent in the pages of science fiction on a journey so immense that its purpose is forgotten until, at the last moment, balance is restored by the response to pre-set stimuli. Boorman takes all these, like fragments of half-remembered folklore, and uses them to set out the theme that lies within all his work – the vital and inevitable impact of one culture on another. As in *Point Blank* or *Deliverance*, the gun in the fist is the symbol of pig-headed virility, its lethal qualities again proving irrelevant as a solution until other, less easy lessons have been learned. And where one of the first images of *Zardoz* has the gun fired directly at the audience, the last shows the weapon hanging forgotten in dust and cobwebs inside the cavernous mouth of the stone God, awaiting a new revolution that may never come.

Birth and rebirth; the film celebrates the perpetuity of life and death with a rational jumble of contradictions, hopes and regrets. At its centre is the extraordinary image of the glass womb, bodies suspended within its liquids in various stages of reconstruction. The creators of the Vortex have abolished death, one of the seldom-defined but always implicit aims of scientific development, and the result should have been a magnificent infinity of refinement and perfection. Instead, the Eternals are without drive or purpose, their heightened mental powers revealing only that the future offers a living extinction. Yearning for death, they eventually find, through Zed, the way to reintroduce it, and in the courageously horrifying conclusion to *Zardoz* a massacre

takes place that is ecstatically welcomed by its victims. Their bodies, splashed with bullet-holes, wriggle life-affirmingly to rest, while Zed retreats to pass on his knowledge without, this time, permitting a machine to do the work instead.

As usual, Boorman keeps up a headlong pace to avoid being crushed by the weight of his argument and the film smashes along like a fist, a dazzling show of conjury that darts between Zed's present predicament and the steps that brought him to it. Superbly photographed by the *2001* cameraman Geoffrey Unsworth, the jolting inferences of Boorman's images are so complex that the first encounter with the film leaves one reeling with questions. But the pieces *do* fit together, and there is a more-than-visual splendour to the scene in which, amid a torrent of lights and colours, Zed is 'educated' by the women of the Vortex as they in turn draw life from him, or the major show-piece of Zed's battle with the super-computer, the diamond 'storage space for refracted light patterns'.

'How,' asks the high priestess of the Vortex, 'did we conjure up a monster in our midst, and why? This is the question we must answer.' In contemporary terms, the question can be applied to any monster you care to think of, from the motor-car to inflation. In science-fiction terms, the answer (we *had* to, in order to survive) was given almost as soon as Mary Shelley had defined the problem; it was then pessimistically reaffirmed by such writers as Carlyle, Kipling and Wells. With *Zardoz*, Boorman demonstrates, Cocteau-fashion, that monsters are not only essential, they are hugely welcome; it's a bold case to make, but he bases it on an irresistible combination of Darwin, Tolkien and the Arthurian legends. And he uses every cinematic trick he can think of, including the engaging talents of a spectacularly good cast, to win us over. Some hints of caricature are there, to be sure, but rhetoric, like science fiction, thrives on exaggeration. As an end-result, *Zardoz* is a luminous and compassionate exploration of what, without our realizing it, has for too long been regarded as unexplorable.

The exploration of the unexplorable. Perhaps, in conclusion, this will serve us for an acceptable definition of the science fiction movie, broad enough to include the vast range between the aliens of our first chapter and the 'unrealities' of our last. In the cinema of the fantastic, the speculative and the surreal, the film-maker satisfies not only the basic requirement of entertainment itself by striving to provide new and fresh experiences but he serves also the very purpose of metaphysics – the human mind's healthy refusal to withdraw from its hopes, fears and dreams. The most voracious human appetite is the imagination – a hunger for exploration, knowledge, and ever-greater miracles. The science fiction movie, stemming from the imagination, stimulates it further. Such is its unique value. And its unique excitement.

INDEX OF FILM TITLES

Figures in italics refer to illustrations